OLD TESTAMENT MESSAGE

A Biblical-Theological Commentary

Carroll Stuhlmueller, C.P. and Martin McNamara, M.S.C.

EDITORS

Old Testament Message, Volume 7

AMOS, HOSEA, MICAH, WITH AN INTRODUCTION TO CLASSICAL PROPHECY

Bruce Vawter, C.M.

Michael Glazier, Inc.
Wilmington, Delaware

First published in 1981 by:
MICHAEL GLAZIER, INC.
1723 Delaware Avenue
Wilmington, Delaware 19806

Distributed outside U.S., Canada & the Philippines by:
GILL & MACMILLAN, LTD.
Goldenbridge, Inchicore
Dublin 8 Ireland

Library of Congress Catalog Card Number: 81-85269
International Standard Book Number
   Old Testament Message series: 0-89453-235-9
   AMOS, HOSEA, MICAH, WITH AN
   INTRODUCTION TO CLASSICAL PROPHECY:
   0-89453-242-1 (Michael Glazier Inc.)
   7171-1171-7 (Gill and Macmillan Ltd.)

Cover design by Lillian Brulc

Printed in the United States of America

CONTENTS

Editors' Preface

Old Testament Message brings into our life and religion today the ancient word of God to Israel. This word, according to the book of the prophet Isaiah, had soaked the earth like "rain and snow coming gently down from heaven" and had returned to God fruitfully in all forms of human life (Isa 55:10). The authors of this series remain true to this ancient Israelite heritage and draw us into the home, the temple and the marketplace of God's chosen people. Although they rely upon the tools of modern scholarship to uncover the distant places and culture of the biblical world, yet they also refocus these insights in a language clear and understandable for any interested reader today. They enable us, even if this be our first acquaintance with the Old Testament, to become sister and brother, or at least good neighbor, to our religious ancestors. In this way we begin to hear God's word ever more forcefully in our own times and across our world, within our prayer and worship, in our secular needs and perplexing problems.

Because life is complex and our world includes, at times in a single large city, vastly different styles of living, we have much to learn from the Israelite Scriptures. The Old Testament spans forty-six biblical books and almost nineteen hundred years of life. It extends through desert, agricultural and urban ways of human existence. The literary style embraces a world of literature and human emotions. Its history began with Moses and the birth-pangs of a new people, it came of age politically and economically under David and Solomon, it reeled under the fiery threats of prophets like Amos and Jeremiah. The people despaired and yet were re-created with new hope during the Babylonian exile. Later reconstruction in the homeland and then the trauma of apocalyptic movements prepared for the revelation of "the mystery hidden for ages in God who created all things" (Eph 3:9).

While the Old Testament telescopes twelve to nineteen hundred years of human existence within the small country of Israel, any single moment of time today witnesses to the reenactment of this entire history across the wide expanse of planet earth. Each verse of the Old Testament is being relived somewhere in our world today. We need, therefore, the *entire* Old Testament and all twenty-three volumes of this new set, in order to be totally a "Bible person" within today's widely diverse society.

The subtitle of this series—"A Biblical-Theological Commentary"—clarifies what these twenty-three volumes intend to do.

Their *purpose* is theological: to feel the pulse of God's word for its *religious* impact and direction.

Their *method* is biblical: to establish the scriptural word firmly within the life and culture of ancient Israel.

Their *style* is commentary: not to explain verse by verse but to follow a presentation of the message that is easily understandable to any serious reader, even if this person is untrained in ancient history and biblical languages.

Old Testament Message—like its predecessor, *New Testament Message*—is aimed at the entire English-speaking world and so is a collaborative effort of an international team. The twenty-one contributors are women and men drawn from North America, Ireland, Britain and Australia. They are scholars who have published in scientific journals, but they have been chosen equally as well for their proven ability to communicate on a popular level. This twenty-three book set comes from Roman Catholic writers, yet, like the Bible itself, it reaches beyond interpretations restricted to an individual church and so enables men and women rooted in biblical faith to unite and so to appreciate their own traditions more fully and more adequately.

Most of all, through the word of God, we seek the blessedness and joy of those

who walk in the law of the Lord!...

who seek God with their whole heart (Ps. 119:1-2).

Carroll Stuhlmueller, C.P.   Martin McNamara, M.S.C.

AN INTRODUCTION TO
CLASSICAL PROPHECY
AND TO
THE BOOKS OF AMOS,
HOSEA, AND MICAH

WHAT IS "CLASSICAL" PROPHECY?

ACCORDING TO the best of our dictionaries, the first meaning of "classical" is "of the first rank of authority; constituting a standard or model; especially in literature." It is undoubtedly in this sense that the term has been applied to the prophetic literature of the Hebrew Old Testament.

When the term was first applied, it was doubtless entirely adequate to its purpose, according to the current wisdom of the time. Nowadays we sense its inadequacies. First of all, it was associated with the notion that the "literary" prophets of Israel—those whose names are traditionally connected with the "books" that appear beneath those names—had written these compositions as so many literary authors, thus distinguishing themselves from other no less genuine prophets (Elijah, Elisha, Micaiah ben Imlah, Nathan, Gad, et al.) who had prophesied indeed but never put pen to paper. We now recognize that this was a false distinction, since it is doubtful that any prophet ever wrote, or wrote very much, that the writing was mainly the result of later reportage, and that some prophets were reported and others were not.

Secondly, it has become apparent that not all literary prophecy is on a par. No single prophetic book is the work, or derives from the work, of any one prophetic genius: all of them are works of redaction and supplementation from many hands, prophetic and otherwise. Sometimes most of the material is anonymous: most of the book of Isaiah, most of the Book of Zechariah, all of Malachi, for random examples. Sometimes it is impossible to determine where the eponymous prophet leaves off—Ezekiel is a good example—and where the epigones have taken over. And even where prophetic names are well founded in the literature, we are not necessarily dealing with the same category of men. Habakkuk, and certainly Nahum, for example, are prophets wholly unlike Amos, Hosea, Isaiah, or Micah. As for the Book of Jonah, though it appears in the list of the Twelve Minor Prophets, it is not a prophetic book at all but rather a didactic work that is, if anything, a kind of gentle parody of prophecy.

Nevertheless, there is a value in preserving the term "classical," if only to distinguish what may be called normative Old Testament prophecy—the prophecy which, rightly or wrongly, has engaged the attention of historians of religion as in a category apart from any other similar phenomenon—from the prophecy which was the common property of the world contemporary with ancient Israel and also otherwise shared by Israel itself. For we must recognize that "prophecy," both in the ancient world and in the present one, is a quite equivocal term.

PROPHECY AND PROPHECY

Everyone is familiar with the story of Tiresias, the blind prophet who revealed to Oedipus, in a somewhat manic fashion according to Sophocles, the circumstances of his past, present, and future. At the background of the Oedipus story lies the influence of the pythonic oracle of Delphi, where the priestess of Apollo, assisted by hallucinosis induced or native, gave vent to babblings which were then "interpreted" by priestly ministrators (who were called *prophetai,* i.e., "those who speak for" someone else). This kind of prophecy depended on "enthusiasm (*en-theos-iasmos* = "a god taking over" in possession) or ecstatic experience (*ek-stasis* = "standing outside" oneself whilst another spirit takes over). This kind of supposed contact with another world that interprets the present is not unknown in the present day and has ancient roots in the age of the Old Testament.

In Mesopotamia an ecstatic priest/prophet of this kind was called a *maḫḫu,*a term which corresponds with the Hebrew *meshuggah* of 2 Kgs 9:11, Jer 29:26, and Hos 9:7. The word means "demented," but we should not be put off by it, since the only meaning was that such persons were driven by an unusual cam, not that they were certifiably dangerous.

Ecstatic priest/prophets existed in Israel as elsewhere in its environs both from its beginnings and well into its "classical" times. Music was a favored means of inducing ecstatic experience particularly in primitive periods (1 Sam 10:5) but also when classical prophecy had taken over (cf. 2 Kgs 3:15). Ecstaticism is an experience which can be genuinely religious, self-manipulative, or simply one of self-delusion. In 1 Kgs 22:20-23 Micaiah ben Imlah, a "classical" prophet, rejects as false the prophecy of Zedekiah ben Chenaanah—an ecstatic prophet—not on the score that he was a deceptive or evil person but rather that he was possessed of a "lying spirit" that had been sent by the Lord. In other words, the visible presence of ecstatic seizure was no longer enough to establish a presumption in favor of divine revelation. At one time, it had been enough.

Another medium of prophecy was divination. The *baru* priests/prophets of Mesopotamia were diviners, and their practice had equivalents throughout the neighboring Near East. Divination was the process of making the present and future revealed by manipulating *things* — by reading the pattern of liquid from a goblet (Gen 44:15), or from a consultation of the livers of newly slaughtered animals, or talismans, or arrows shaken out at random (cf. Ezek 21:23-28). In later Israelite law divination was strictly prohibited (e.g., Deut 18:10-11); nevertheless, its practice remained widespread (cf. Isa 2:6). For Jeremiah, those whom he calls "prophets of peace" and whom we frequently know as "false prophets," are equated with "diviners" (cf. 14:13-16). Still, an "orthodox" form of divination has been retained in the Urim and Thummim which the Priestly source of the Pentateuch (Exod 28:30; Lev 8:8) ascribes to the high priest. Earlier biblical sources (e.g., Deut 33:8; 1 Sam 28:6) indicate the common and quite routine use made of such devices in more remote times.

A third prophetic medium was the dream. A reader of the Bible, Old or New Testament, will recall how often dreams occur there as the means of divine revelation, whether this be achieved by oneiromancy (the professional interpretation of another's dreams, as by a Joseph or a Daniel) or by direct communication with the Deity which the recipient acquires through his own dream. It is interesting to note in the documents of Mari, that city on the Euphrates river which during the eighteenth century B.C.

managed to produce some prophetic phenomena strikingly similar to those later found in biblical tradition, dreams appear to have been the preferred medium of private prophecy as distinct from the ecstaticism and divination characteristic of the official sanctuary prophecy of which we have spoken above. Interesting, because the classical prophecy of Israel is more readily identifiable as private than as having an official character at court or temple.There are exceptions to this rule, of course, but episodes like Amos 7:10-17, 1 Kgs 22:1-28, and the whole career of Jeremiah, to mention only three, certainly illustrate the rule. Interesting, too, because the term most habitually associated with this classical prophecy to designate the means by which it was communicated is that of "vision," and dreams are at least one way by which vision was to be had.

It is true, dreams are often connected with prophecy that is false and misguided (cf. Jer 23:25-32, 27:9, 29:8-9). Dreamer, diviner, magician can be condemned in one breath as reprehensible persons devoted to forbidden rites. Doubtless the dreamer sometimes resorted to the practice called incubation, dreaming his dreams in the vicinity of or within tombs, on the superstitious premise that esoteric knowledge was to be acquired by consulting the dead (cf. 1 Sam 28:8-19). Necromancy in any form was also a forbidden practice. Nevertheless, a passage like Deut 13:2-6 indicates that "dreamer" could be a perfectly acceptable synonym for "prophet" with no pejorative connotations.

It is true, however, that dreams were by no means the only way, or even the primary way, in which prophetic vision occurred. As a matter of fact, even though dreams are frequently mentioned in the Bible as the vehicle of divine revelation, only infrequently are they explicitly tied to prophetic vision (e.g., Joel 3:1-2; *RSV* 2:28-29). We may find them implied on occasion, or some trancelike experience similar to dreams. Many of the visions of Ezekiel, for example, which he ascribes to the hand or spirit of the Lord descending upon him, lifting him up, and transporting him from place to place, have suggested to some commentators the product of dreams or perhaps ecstatic experience. Other visions, however, like those of an Amos or a Jeremiah, appear to have been the result simply of some special insight or clairvoyance, by which the prophet was enabled to see through the observation of something as routine as a locust swarm or a boiling pot a significance which was for him the word of God. In Arab tradition a clairvoyant of this kind was called a *kahin,* a word cognate with the Hebrew *kohen,* "priest," a reminder of the early identification of the priestly and prophetic functions. In short, the process of the "vision" by which the prophet "saw" the word of God, to use some of the most typical language with which the Bible describes the prophetic experience, was doubtless quite varied, differed from prophet to prophet and from interval to interval in the prophet's career, and it is highly unlikely that any amount of study will ever permit us to reduce it to one common denominator.

THE *NABI* IN ISRAEL

The corollary of vision is the seer, "the one who sees" (*hozeh* or *roeh*). According to 1 Sam 9:9, "seer" was the earlier designation for what Israel came later to call "prophet" (*nabi*). Other terms are used, among them "man of God" (1 Sam 2:27, etc.), "man of the spirit" (Hos 9:7), "messenger of the Lord" (Isa 44:26, etc.), "servant of God" (Jer 7:25, etc.). But *nabi* came to be the standard, catch-all title. The etymology and original meaning of the Hebrew word are disputed and unknown. The Septuagint translators, from whom we have inherited most of our biblical terminology, rendered it *prophetes* ("spokesperson"), hence our "prophet." It is well that they did so, avoiding terms like *mantis* by which prophets were better known in the Greek world, referring to the *mania* or ecstatic frenzy in which oracles were delivered at shrines like Delphi; such a designation would have been inappropriate for the classical prophets of Israel. However, this uniform translation merely perpetuated the ambiguity already present in the Bible's Hebrew usage. In the Hebrew there is not even an adjectival means of distinguishing a false prophet from a true one, or one kind of prophet from another. It was the Septuagint translation, again, that introduced the term "pseudoprophet," and that only in a few cases, notably in the book of Jeremiah.

Prophecy in Israel may be compared with "wisdom" in Israel or cultic worship in Israel. All three came to Israel from without, were absorbed by it and ultimately transformed by it. The transformation, however, required a history, and in this history there was no straight line of development. Prophets of an "older" stripe continued to coexist with newer prophetic movements, and a prophet of one school might not willingly identify himself with those of another. This, as we shall see below, is probably the explanation of Amos 7:14. The assertion of Amos here would otherwise seem strange, when he disclaims being either prophet or prophet's son.

The historical books of Israel presuppose prophecy to be a well established institution at the time of Israel's entry into nationhood, even though "the word of the Lord was rare in those days; there was no frequent vision" (1 Sam 3:1). About prophecy in the earlier tribal society we have no reliable information. Later tradition ascribed the institution of prophecy to Moses (Num 11:24-30), just as it tended to ascribe to him all of Israel's institutions. The prophecy described there seems to have been modelled on the visible, ecstatic kind. Similarly, the prophets over whom Samuel presided and whose spirit also infected Saul and his messengers appear to have been of the ecstatic kind (1 Sam 19:18-24). It has been suggested that not by chance does the tradition associate these prophets with the location of a Philistine garrison (1 Sam 10:5), that in other words their ability to generate enthusiasm was pressed into the service of Israel's nationalist wars. The text just mentioned notes the presence of instrumental music which doubtless assisted and accompanied the ecstatic experience. The same practice is later associated with the prophet Elisha (2 Kgs 3:15), who was also leader of a band of "sons of the prophets" (2 Kgs 4:1, 9:1, etc.), those who formed a prophetic guild or were "apprentice" prophets.

In the early days of the monarchy the prophets Gad (also called "the seer") and Nathan are closely associated with David's rise to power and with his court. Their role was that of royal counsellors, assisted by prophetic vision, sometimes apparently in the form of dreams (cf. 2 Sam 7:4). David also could "consult the Lord" by a modified form of divination ministered by the priest Abiathar (1 Sam 23:6-12, etc.). In the consolidation of David's dynasty and transmission of the succession to Solomon, Nathan appears as the perfect court prophet, forerunner of the four hundred of 1 Kgs 22:5-12 and the authors of some of the "royal" Psalms, to whom nation and loyalty to the throne were paramount. Yet in 2 Sam 12:1-12 Nathan assumes the guise of a classical prophet like Isaiah or Jeremiah in his fearless denunciation of the abuses of royal power.

With the separation of the kingdoms after Solomon, the sources tell of prophets both in the north and south, though we are better informed about the northern situation, a fact which probably testifies to an older and firmer prophetic tradition in Israel than in Judah. Unfortunately, these sources are not of such a character as to give us the historical information we might like. In part, they reflect viewpoints that are hardly contemporary but rather belong to later times. The Elijah and Elisha cycles of the books of Kings devote considerable attention to these northern prophets, but much of it is concerned with the reputation of wonder-workers with which popular tradition had surrounded them. These cycles also stress the heavy involvement, even intervention, of the prophets in politics—a feature which a disinterested historian might be disposed to judge more negatively than do the biblical writers. On the other hand, Elijah who like Elisha is associated with bands of cultic or nationalistic "sons of the prophets" (2 Kgs 2:7, etc.), is also represented in 1 Kgs 21:17-24 defending the common man against royal rapacity with all the vigor of an Amos or a Hosea. Towards the end of the chronicle, 2 Kgs 19:20-20:19 treats the prophet Isaiah somewhat in the manner of an Elijah or an Elisha, though Isaiah is in the counsel of a good rather than a bad king. Some of the descriptions of prophets and prophetic activity, such as those of 1 Kgs 13:1-32, are in part puzzling and doubtless speak to concerns that are now obscure. In short, the long period before the appearance of "literary" prophecy seems to have been played out in the company of just about every variety of prophet that has been mentioned above. There were also prophetesses, like the Huldah of 2 Kgs 22:14-20.

"LITERARY" PROPHECY

Though not, as we have seen, wholly unheralded, the prophecy of Israel's coming judgment that begins with Amos and is continued by his successors catches the reader of the Bible quite by surprise. He is not really prepared for it by anything and everything that has gone before.

"Literary" prophecy, we have already said, is another of

those terms that derive from an out-of-date conception of the process by which Israel's prophetic word has been transmitted to subsequent generations. The thought was that, while for knowledge of the teaching of earlier prophets like Nathan, Elijah, Micaiah ben Imlah, and a host of others, we were dependent on third-person narration that had been gathered into the tradition, from the time of Amos and thereafter we have the prophets' own words written by their own hands. There may be some validity still attaching to this "literary" designation, reflecting the transition of Israel from a professionally literate into a generally literate society—a matter that can be the subject of much debate. But we now recognize that although these later prophets may indeed have written on occasion and certainly on occasion had their words written down for them (cf. Isa 8:16, Jeremiah 36 and 45, etc.), for the most part they have been preserved to us through the agency of their disciples who are responsible for most of the writing, including third-person material that continued to be recorded.

The real distinction between Amos and his predecessors has little to do with the literary or non-literary transmission of the prophetic message. Admittedly we might have to modify this judgment were we in as much a direct contact with the predecessors as we are with Amos. On the other hand, there is no reason that the pre-classical prophets' words should not have been preserved as carefully as were those of the classical prophets, had the words been deemed worth the preservation for their own and later generations. Prophetic disciples, we have seen, were not lacking in pre-classical times. By the same token, the classical prophets could hardly have been the isolated, lonely figures they sometimes appear, since it is upon their disciples that we have from them what we have. It seems to have been a matter of different interests, a different ethos, different conceptions of the function of prophecy. The real distinction between Amos and his predecessors rises from a different idea of the prophetic role in Israel and of the content of the prophetic word, both qualitatively and quantitatively.

Qualitative, first. With prophets of the Amos type Israelite prophecy reaches full term in the assimilation of the prophetic experience to the best traditions of the Yahwistic religion. It is now that, for all practical purposes, Israelite prophecy ceases to have parallels in the prophecy of the surrounding cultures and religions. As happened virtually nowhere else, prophecy in Israel became a conscience for the nation and the people, no longer offering assurance of victory to its kings and officials but reading them words of judgment and doom, criticizing and condemning the institutions of court and sanctuary within which it had grown up and with which it still maintained some form of contact. In the process it so married the practice of religion to individual moral conduct that forever after the two have been inseparable in the Judeo-Christian mind—a combination that hithertofore was not always generally accepted and is still not accepted in some other religious traditions. Quantitatively, too. We must not exaggerate, for there were good and decent men and women in other contemporary societies who had perceptions like those of Israel's prophets. But the continuity and consistency are lacking. There is nothing to equal the intensity with which Israelite classical prophecy pursued its goal, from the beginning to the end of the monarchy, from the beginning to the end of Israel as an autonomous nation.

A final word should be spoken, about the end of Israelite prophecy. Particularly during the exile and afterwards, when Israel had suffered the punishments which earlier prophets had confidently predicted, consolation and visions of a glorious future become the heart of the prophetic message. These visions, too, depend on the best of Israel's traditions, but while they would have been singularly inappropriate in the days of Israel's pride, they were quite proper in the time of humiliation and degradation. They, too, are the product of classical prophecy. They appear already with some of the exilic prophets, they are especially evident in the prophets who tried to help in the rebuilding of Israel after the exile, and they also account for numberless additions to the preexilic prophetic books, all of which have been edited from postexilic viewpoints. We shall point out these additions in the commentary below.

There is really no adequate accounting for the phenomenon of classical Israelite prophecy within its age and within its environment. We do not attempt to account for it now, other than to have described its rise and its character. The prophets themselves ascribed it simply to the power of the Lord. For those who believe that there is something very special about biblical religion, only this explanation will suffice.

The introductions which follow contain certain preliminary information that will be useful in the reading and study of the prophets Amos, Hosea, and Micah. Other such information that is frequently found in introductions will be found to have been incorporated into the commentaries.

Introduction to Amos

The Prophet

Practically nothing can be known about the prophet Amos, his background, even the circumstances of his prophecy itself, except for what can be extracted from the book which bears his name. Some of those particulars are reserved for the commentary below. The period of his prophecy was probably about 760-750 B.C. He came from Tekoa, a Judahite village in the neighborhood of Bethlehem, though his prophetic mission appears to have taken him exclusively to the northern kingdom of Israel. In Israel, the scenes of his activity are certainly the royal shrine of Bethel and possibly also the capital city of Samaria. From these different scenes and what they perceive as a difference of interests, some authors have concluded to the presence of two prophets, two "Amoses" at work in this book, besides the anonymous prophets who are responsible for the additions to which it has been subjected. In the commentary that follows we hold to the view of a single Amos with consistent interests.

Amos prophesies against the backdrop of Israel's greatest territorial expansion, nationalist enthusiasm, and material affluence. It was a time of complacency, self-satisfaction, conspicuous consumption, and comfortable religiosity. This much we might have known, or surmised, from our other sources of information. It is to Amos, and, to a less extent, to Hosea, that we look for social commentary on the scene. It is these prophets who have told us how all this prosperity was façade covering official corruption and apathy, a callous disregard for basic human rights, and a system that reduced the poor and defenseless to a state of peonage. The great society guaranteed the comfort of the few at the expense of the misery of the many.

Amos thus becomes the first of Israel's social prophets. He would not be the last.

The Text

The Hebrew text of the book of Amos is one of the best preserved in the Bible. This fact has both made its translation relatively easy and probably testifies to an early acceptance of the work as in some sense canonical, a work which was handed down with more than the usual textual care.

The work as it stands is the product of postexilic redaction. That is to say, words of and about the prophet which were preserved by his disciples have been codified by later editors into some sort of logical order and adapted to conditions and viewpoints subsequent to those of Amos. An outline of the work follows:

Title (1:1)
Exordium (1:2)
Oracles against the nations (1:3-2:5)
and against Israel (2:6-16)
Indictments of Israel (3:1-6:14)
Visions (7:1-9)
Biographical Interlude (7:10-17)
Vision of the summer fruit (8:1-3)
Indictment of Israel continued (8:4-14)
Vision of the altar (9:1-6)
Indictment of Israel concluded (9:7-10)
Redactional conclusion (9:11-15)

Introduction to Hosea

The Prophet

About Hosea we have even less information than we do about Amos. Even if the initial three chapters of the book do refer to a definite experience in the prophet's life, a view that is adopted in this commentary, they really do not tell us a great deal about him in the way of biographic data. On the other hand, in his prophetic words he has probably revealed more about himself indirectly, his feelings and sensitivity, his sense of priorities, than any other prophet with the exception of Jeremiah. These traits we shall examine below in the commentary.

He seems to have begun to prophesy towards the end of

the reign of Jeroboam II, say about 748 B.C. The time when his prophecy ended is much more difficult to determine. Much of his prophecy appears to reflect the anarchy that accompanied the dissolution of the kingdom, but this dissolution was long and drawn out. He was probably still active when the Assyrians were at Israel's door signalling its end around 725, but it is doubtful that he saw the final blow fall in the occupation of Samaria in 721.

Hosea was a northern Israelite. His prophecies regard northern sites, and his familiarity with the northern scene is that of a native. He lived during the dismantlement of the little empire that had been predicted by Amos, and in this general breakdown he was confronted by different problems than those which Amos had observed and which required somewhat different responses, including above all that of compassion. One gains the impression that Hosea was a far more sensitive man than Amos, more balanced, but also perhaps more distanced from the rough and tumble that gives such poignancy to Amos' prophecies. At all events, his interests were broader and his judgments more nuanced. Hosea held out hope for Israel whereas Amos held out none. Much of what is distinctive about Hosea, it may be suggested, is explicable in terms of the prophetic experience described in chaps. 1-3.

The Text

The Hebrew text of Hosea holds the distinction of being possibly the worst preserved of all the books of the Old Testament. This state of affairs makes translation particularly difficult and accounts for the considerable differences that one is likely to detect from one vernacular version to another. The first three chapters have a more secure textual transmission than does the rest of the book.

The book falls into two unequal parts, chaps. 1-3 on the one hand and chaps. 4-14 on the other. It is pointless to attempt an outline of these parts. Hosea's book, like the other prophetic works, is a product of redaction, but while there are obvious considerations of content that have dictated the division of the two parts, no one has ever been able to offer to the satisfaction of anyone else the rationale by which Hosea's prophecies concerning Israel in chaps. 4-14 have been gathered and ordered. The descriptive headings which we have employed in the commentary to facilitate the discussion of the text part by part will have to serve as our only outline.

Introduction to Micah

The Prophet

Micah—the name is a shortening of Micaiah, "who is like Yahweh?"—was a prophet from Moresheth or Moresheth-gath, a little village in the Shephelah or foothills of Judah, who prophesied in the days of Hezekiah the king (Jer 26:18). From internal evidence we can conclude that his prophetic career began at the latest around 725 B.C., the beginning of the final days of the northern kingdom of Israel, and it ended at its earliest probably around 701 B.C., the time of the investment of Jerusalem by the Assyrian king Sennacherib.

Micah, therefore, was a contemporary of Isaiah in Judah. That neither prophet had occasion to advert to the other is not remarkable, since the lack of such reference is the rule rather than the exception in the prophetic books. Furthermore, while Isaiah was a city man through and through, closely bound to the sacred traditions of Jerusalem and obviously highly placed in its society, Micah was just as obviously a man of the countryside, close to the victims of the disorders whose wellsprings were in

Jerusalem. Micah and Isaiah thus complement each other. They complement each other not only in their basic agreement from different vantage points about what was wrong with Judah and what its inevitable destiny was soon to be, but also, again from somewhat different premises and points of departure, in their appeal to ancient traditions which offered consolation for the repentant. Both the negative and the positive of Micah's prophecy will be seen in the commentary below.

Unfortunately, no further particulars about Micah are to be had other than from his gathered prophecies. Any attempt to determine his social standing or other background can rely only on sheer speculation.

The Text

The Hebrew text of this book rivals that of Hosea in testifying to a bad state of preservation.

Not unconnected with this fact, perhaps, has been the critical proclivity to question the Mican authenticity of large parts of the book and to assign them to the hands of later supplementers and redactors. Not too long ago, only the first three chapters (and those not in their entirety) and some of chap. 7 were considered by some scholars to be the work of the eighth-century prophet; all else was alien to him. But criticism has mellowed, or rather it has become more sophisticated and less prone to the application of peremptory criteria. Certainly there are non-Mican sections of the book, which is a work of later editing like all the others in the prophetic collections. But they are far fewer than was once thought, and each must be considered individually and without prior judgment. In the commentary those sections will be discussed one by one.

An outline of the book would go like this:

Title (1:1)

Judgment on Israel and Judah (1:2-2:11)

Restoration (2:12-13)
Judgment on Judah's rulers (chap. 3)
Jerusalem: future glory, present shame (4:1-5:1)
Messianic texts (5:2-9)
Judgment on Judah continued (5:10-15)
Yahweh's lawsuit (6:1-8)
Indictment of Jerusalem (6:9-7:7)
The restoration of Zion (7:8-20)

The Commentary

AMOS

THE TITLE
1:1

> **1** The words of Amos, who was among the shepherds of Tekoa, which he saw concerning Israel in the days of Uzziah king of Judah and in the days of Jeroboam the son of Joash, king of Israel, two years before the earthquake.

THE DATES assigned to the "writing" prophets in these titles are almost invariably the guesses of later Judahite editors who correlated them according to their knowledge of the concurrent reigns of Israelite kings of the south and of the north. In the present case, there is, however, little doubt that the editors were correct in assigning Amos to the time of Jeroboam II of Israel (786-746 B.C.): for that there is the internal evidence of Amos 7:10-17. We can probably be even more precise. Commentators have long relied on a plausible assumption that Amos 8:9 recalled the experience of a total eclipse of the sun and have therefore closely associated the prophecy of Amos with a total eclipse that would have been visible in Palestine on 15 June 763. Furthermore, the earthquake of which the title speaks—obviously an occurrence closely associated with Amos' prophecy—may be another chronological pointer, despite the fact that earthquakes have been and are fairly frequent in Palestine. There was, it appears, a notable one that occurred there about 760 B.C. These positive data may confirm the impression conveyed by the content of this prophecy, that we are dealing with the period of the second half of Jeroboam II's reign following on his imperialistic "restoration" of Israel's boundaries (cf. 2 Kgs 14:25) which guaranteed a wealth for the privileged classes that was bought at the expense of a new category of people which in modern terms would have to be called a rural proletariat.

Amos is said to have been "among the shepherds of Tekoa." Tekoa was a city in Judah more or less half-way between Jerusalem to the south and Bethel to the north in the kingdom of Israel: it is likely that these few sites made up the totality of the area that witnessed Amos' prophetic activity. The word translated here "shepherd" is found elsewhere only in 2 Kgs 3:4 where it applies to Mesha, the king of Moab. In neither place did the ancient Greek translation of the Hebrew Bible understand the meaning of this word. While it probably does, indeed, mean "shepherd," it was in all likelihood more a social than an occupational term. There is evidence from the usage of other contemporary languages that it had to do with some kind of official standing (not necessarily connected with the temple or sanctuary, as had sometimes been thought). The idea that Amos himself belonged to the humble and deprived classes whose cause he defended is an old one, but based only on supposition.

AN EXORDIUM
1:2

> [2] And he said:
> "The Lord roars from Zion,
> and utters his voice from Jerusalem;

and pastures of the shepherds mourn,
and the top of Carmel withers."

There is no reason to question the fact that these are
Amos' words, but there is good reason to suspect that an
editor of his prophecies has taken these words, remembered from some perhaps rather specific historical circumstance, and made them into something like a leitmotiv to
characterize the prophecy that follows. For there is no doubt
that Amos is, above all, a prophet inspired by faith in the
Yahweh of Judah and Jerusalem, a God who, at the same
time, exercises judgment not only over northern Israel
(Carmel), but over the rest of the world as well. Probably
the "mourn" of the pasturages in this verse should be better translated "dry up": in keeping with prophetic theology, acts of God were interpreted as visitations for popular iniquity. Here a drought and a deforestation seem to be
in view. Carmel today is a bleak hillside, but once it sup-
ported a lush growth.

JUDGMENT OF THE NATIONS
1:3-2:8

³ Thus says the Lord
   "For three transgressions of Damascus,
   and for four, I will not revoke the punishment;
   because they have threshed Gilead
      with threshing sledges of iron.
⁴ So I will send a fire upon the house of Hazael,
      and it shall devour the strongholds of Ben-hadad.
⁵ I will break the bar of Damascus,
   and cut off the inhabitants from the Valley of Aven,
   and him that holds the scepter from Beth-eden;
   and the people of Syria shall go into exile to Kir,"
                                             says the Lord.

This is the longest of all the oracles about the nations that follow in this series, and certain things should be noted. (1) First of all, are these verses a unity originally produced by the prophet, or is this complex due to later editorial work? Much speaks in favor of there being here at least a nucleus of an original prophetic pronouncement that would have had a striking rhetorical effect. (2) The "numerical ladder" form ("for three. . . for four"), an oral or literary device common to other Old Testament literature (cf. Prov 30:15-31, etc.) and cognate sources, simply means, in this case at least, an indeterminate number. (3) The "sin" in question ("transgressions" is a prophetic word which almost invariably signifies violation of the covenant of God) is in every case, whether directed against Israel or not, something inhumane and unconscionable, a crime against humanity. (4) It is assumed, for whatever reason, that the Yahweh of Israel can call to count for their crimes against humanity the Arameans of the north who worship an alien God. The importance of this element will become more apparent as the series develops.

> [6] Thus says the Lord:
>   "For three transgressions of Gaza,
>   and for four, I will not revoke the punishment;
>   because they carried into exile a whole people
>   to deliver them up to Edom.
> [7] So I will send a fire upon the wall of Gaza,
>   and it shall devour her strongholds.
> [8] I will cut off the inhabitants from Ashdod,
>   and him that holds the scepter from Ashkelon;
>   I will turn my hand against Ekron;
>   and the remnant of the Philistines shall perish,"
>   says the Lord God.

Amos' attention is now directed to the south, towards Philistia. Like Aram to the north, the Philistines were typical enemies of Israel, and an Israelite prophet could be assured of an eager audience of Israelites when he embarked upon a roll call of the vices of those who had abused the nation and the nation's God. Yet an attentive listener should already have become aware that something other than a routine appeal to chauvinistic pride was being expected from this strange prophet from Judah. True, in the case of Aram he had denounced transgressions that had involved Gilead—part of northern Israel. But now the question rises, was Amos' condemnation of Aram so much motivated by its having devastated Israel or its having, in any case, perpetrated barbarous, inhumane acts? For the accusation against Philistia does not obviously involve anything specifically Judahite (and Judah was as much the "enemy" of Israel as was Philistia), much less Israelite. Philistia was the enclave of the Philistines, a non-Semitic people who had invaded the land of Canaan from the sea at about the same time Israel was being formed there through a combination of tribal invasions from the south and east combined with a polarization of indigenous Semitic populations. The Philistines inhabited their enclave all the lifetime of the united kingdom and the separate kingdoms of Israel and Judah. At one time, before the reign of David, they had threatened to dominate the land entirely (1 Samuel 31; 2 Sam 8:1). Lately this had not been so. Nevertheless, they remained a powerful, mercantile people, a nation of entrepreneurs. They had once held a monopoly on the import of precious iron, which spelled the difference between survival and defeat both in war and in agriculture (1 Sam 13:19-22). It is another of the Philistines' businesses that Amos finds condemnable: traffic in slaves on a large scale. Slavery in its milder forms (family retainers, indentured debtors) was taken for granted in Israel's contemporary society, but selling human beings into slavery against their will was regarded as kidnaping and a detestable practice punishable by death (Exod 21:16, Deut 24:7), and a runaway slave who had fled his master was not to be returned to him (Deut 23:16-17).

As in the case of Aram, Amos signifies the coming judgment on Philistia by predicting the devastation of its chief cities. It is interesting that of the famed Philistine pentapolis, the most famous of all the cities—Gath—is not named here while all four others are. Perhaps Gath was already thought to have received its punishment in view of the conquest and razing of its walls by Uzziah of Judah (2 Chr 26:6). Elsewhere in Amos (6:2) Gath appears as a byword for a place that has known destruction.

> [9] Thus says the Lord:
> "For three transgressions of Tyre,
>   and for four, I will not revoke the punishment;
> because they delivered up a whole people to Edom,
>   and did not remember the covenant of brotherhood.
> [10] So I will send a fire upon the wall of Tyre,
>   and it shall devour her strongholds."

There are good reasons to suspect that this and the following oracle against Edom do not derive from Amos himself but were later added in his spirit to fill out the specifics of his indictment. These critical considerations need not deter us from our purpose to comment on the canonical text, which in any case is not affected by them as regards the message of Amos or of his book.

Tyre, the island fortress off the shore of Phoenicia, was not humbled by foreign investment till a century and a half after Amos' time; whereupon, in later prophetic texts (Isaiah 23; Jer 25:22, Ezek 26:15; Zech 9:3-4), it became proverbial as an example of how the high and mighty could be brought low by the power of divine retribution. Here

Tyre stands for the kingdom of Phoenicia, allied with Israel ("the convenant of brotherhood") under Solomon (1 Kgs 9:13), an alliance that was repeatedly reconfirmed with the northern kingdom long before Amos. The crime with which Phoenicia is here charged is essentially that ascribed to the Philistines above. "Aram" rather than "Edom" (the two words are quite similar in the Hebrew spelling) might be thought geographically the better option for those to whom the Phoenicians—a mercantile people like the Philistines—would more likely have sold their slaves. But "Edom," if indeed "Edom" was what the author originally wrote, adds a further dimension to the enormity of the crime if we assume, as seems indicated by the context, that the slaves he had in mind were Israelites. The additional dimension would be that of selling brother to brother, Israelite to Edomite.

> [11] Thus says the Lord:
>   "For three transgressions of Edom,
>   and for four, I will not revoke the punishment;
>   because he pursued his brother with the sword,
>   and cast off all pity,
>   and his anger tore perpetually,
>   and he kept his wrath for ever.
> [12] So I will send a fire upon Teman,
>   and it shall devour the strongholds of Bozrah."

The indictment of Edom is only sketchily specified. Vaguely, Edom is accused of ferocious and predatory conduct against "his brother," which can only be Israel. The earliest of Israelite historical traditions connected Israelites with Edomites as blood relations (Gen 25:19-34). From the standpoint of political history, Edom, a Semitic kingdom with pre-Israelite roots (Genesis 36), was first subjugated by David and incorporated into his little empire (2 Sam 8:13-14). After the separation of the kingdoms of Judah and Israel it remained in Judahite control, off and on, till well after the time of Amos. Struggles between Judah and Edom in the interim doubtless accounted on both sides for the kind of atrocities that these verses seem to suppose. However, it was only after 586 B.C., after the Chaldean invasion that levelled Jerusalem and devastated Judah, that the Edomites were able to move in as jackals and prey on their brothers in quite the fashion that is described here. This fact, together with the other that the abhorrence here expressed is at least as much nationalistic as it is humanitarian, might suggest that the text is a later expansion of Amos' prophecy. Teman and Bozrah were for Israelites "traditional" Edomite names, of uncertain location.

> [13] Thus says the Lord:
>   For three transgressions of the Ammonites,
>   and for four, I will not revoke the punishment;
>   because they have ripped up women with child in
>   Gilead,
>   that they might enlarge their border,
> [14] So I will kindle a fire in the wall of Rabbah,
>   and it shall devour her strongholds,
>   with shouting in the day of battle,
>   with a tempest in the day of the whirlwind;
> [15] and their king shall go into exile,
>   he and his princes together,"
>
> says the Lord.

With this oracle we seem to be once again on firm Amosian ground. Both the Ammonites and the Moabites who are the subject of the following oracles were peoples with whom the Israelites acknowledged a remote common ancestry (Gen 19:30-38), but whom history and circumstance had completely sundered from Israel. The law of Deut 23:4 forbade entry into the Israelite community of any Ammonite or Moabite or of their blood descent down to the tenth generation. The crime of which the Ammonites are charged is, again, one perpetrated against Israelites. No matter that it was a crime of which Israelites were equally capable (2 Kgs 15:16). In view of what the prophet is about to charge against Israel, it is evident that the inhumane act itself, by whomever the culprit, was the object of his detestation. That it was charged against Ammon, of course, a hated enemy, would have furthered his rhetorical purpose, to allow Israel eventually to recognize that "we have met the enemy, and they is us," or, in more traditional biblical language: "You are the man" (2 Sam 12:7).

Rabbah, the capital of the Ammonites mentioned in v 14, is shorthand for Rabbath Ammon, "the great city of the Ammonites." It remains today, after many transformations, as the city of Amman, the capital of the Hashemite Kingdom of the Jordan. In v 15 the ancient versions of the Hebrew text suggest interesting variations on the precise character of the Ammonite leadership that was doomed for exile, but these variations are not important enough to be followed up here.

> **2** Thus says the Lord:
> "For three transgressions of Moab,
>   and for four, I will not revoke the punishment;
> because he burned to lime
>   the bones of the king of Edom.
> [2] So I will send a fire upon Moab,
>   and it shall devour the strongholds of Kerioth,

> and Moab shall die amid uproar,
> amid shouting and the sound of the trumpet;
> ³ I will cut off the ruler from its midst,
> and will slay all its princes with him,"
>
> says the Lord.

Modern commentators have found an incongruity between what had previously been registered as a crime against humanity and what is now charged against Moab in v 1. "Because he burned the bones of the king of Edom": this is in the Hebrew *'al-śorĕpô 'aṣmôt melek-'ĕdôm*. It could also be read, with a slight change of vowels in the last two words (vowels were not supplied in the original Hebrew text), *'al-śorĕpô 'aṣmôt mōlek-'ādām,* which would mean, presumably, "because he burnt the bones of a human sacrifice." However, it is probable that this proposed "correction" of the Hebrew text owes more to modern sensibilities than it does to attunement with the spirit of Amos. Human sacrifice, it is true, was not proper Israelite practice in Amos' time; it was, nevertheless, so common a practice in contemporary society (Genesis 22; Mic 6:7), a practice in societies superior in many respects to that of Israel, that it would not have provoked the revulsion that it would nowadays with one of us. On the other hand, desecration of a person's dead body was an unthinkable crime against humanity (2 Kgs 23:16-18; Ps 79:3, etc.). Whatever may have been the religious taboo underlying this prohibition, it remains that a violation of it would have been considered an enormity. Add to this the fact it was the bones of the king of Edom which were so treated. We have no way of knowing to what historical event the text may have made reference. Edom was never a friend to Israel, nor was Moab, but what Moab had done to Edom in this instance contravened a common Semitic prescription to which Israelites and Judahites were equally subject.

If the earlier lines of this oracle encourage us to think that we are, indeed, here hearing Amos' voice, the last lines are not too encouraging of this belief. The conclusion is rather perfunctory. The "strongholds" (cf. 1:7, 10, 12, 14) of Moab are doomed, which are summed up in Kerioth, a word which means "cities," which are not otherwise specified.

> ⁴ Thus says the Lord:
>   "For three transgressions of Judah,
>   and for four, I will not revoke the punishment;
>   because they have rejected the law of the Lord,
>   and have not kept his statutes,
>   but their lies have led them astray,
>   after which their fathers walked.
> ⁵ So I will send a fire upon Judah,
>   and it shall devour the strongholds of Jerusalem."

There can be no doubt here. These verses have obviously been added at a later date to bring Amos' prophecy into line with a later theology. The passage merely imitates the preceding oracles in form, while it departs from them substantively in content. Judah is condemned in totally Deuteronomic language of having abandoned the *torah,* of having violated the precepts of the Law, and of having pursued idolatry ("their lies"). The passage loses nothing of its religious value for having been a supplement to Amos' message. When the Israel of the north where Amos had first preached had eventually disappeared in fulfillment of his prophecy (about 721 B.C.), the word of the prophet descended down to Judah, his native land, and was adapted there to the southrons whose problems were not all that different from those of their compatriots to the north. (See the commentary on Micah below.) This passage, however, does not address such earlier problems: a good indication that it derives from a far later time. Obedience to the letter of the Law, abhorrence of every suggestion of idolatry, such are the hallmarks of a later Judaism, insinuating rules and regulations that never needed to be formulated in an earlier age when "the true religion" required of its faithful adherents only certain moral precepts inherent in a covenant that had been made between a God and a people, an internal thing, rather than an orthodoxy of belief measured against foreign contamination.

> [6] Thus says the Lord:
>   "For three transgressions of Israel,
>   and for four, I will not revoke the punishment;
>   because they sell the righteous for silver,
>   and the needy for a pair of shoes—
> [7] they that trample the head of the poor
>   into the dust of the earth,
>   and turn aside the way of the afflicted;
>   a man and his father go in to the same maiden,
>   so that my holy name is profaned;
> [8] they lay themselves down beside every altar
>   upon garments taken in pledge;
>   and in the house of their God they drink
>   the wine of those who have been fined.

The climax of what we conceive to have been an original rhetorical unity has now been reached. If Amos' Israelite auditors had been pleased to hear the rehearsal of their enemies' vices from this strange prophetic figure, now at least they must have come to the realization that they had been beguiled into a false sense of complacency. What Amos was now telling them was that they were guilty of the selfsame sins of their Gentile neighbors, fratricidal crimes against a common humanity. Perhaps not all of those who heard Amos, however, would have necessarily been displeased by what he said. Some of them, who had suffered the depredations which the prophet was now denouncing, might have found it a novel thing that violations of human rights were being excoriated from the same pulpit from which they were used to hearing routine endorsements of the policies of authority and establishment, especially in this "king's sanctuary and temple of the kingdom" (7:13).

There are, apparently, in these verses two specifics being charged against the high and mighty in Israel that amount to an intolerable oppression that they were imposing upon the bulk of the Israelite nation. Firstly, the courts of justice had been corrupted (cf. 5:10-13). The "righteous" (read, "the innocent") were being convicted for money, for "a pair of shoes" (read, "for a bribe"). It was the poor and afflicted who made up this corps of the oppressed. The new proletariat were the victims of a system that was rigged against them. The privileged were, in contrast, flaunting themselves by sanctimoniously holding forth in the holy places on festal occasions reclining on the garments that the poor had forfeited as surety for their debts (Exod 22:24-26; Deut 24:12-13) and feasting on the wine that had been drawn from their veins by means of exactions over which the exploiters held complete control.

Secondly, "a man and his father go in to the same maiden." It has been thought that Amos was here condemning the cult prostitution which had penetrated Israelite religious practice in imitation of Canaanite practices that surrounded them (see the commentary on Hosea below). But this is not too likely, in view of the little interest that Amos evinces in cultic practices in general. Rather, it seems that he is thinking simply of the poor, unprotected, unmarried girl who could easily become the prey of any "squire" of the neighborhood and his son, were there no law or custom to protect her. Later Israelite law (Leviticus 18) spelled out various rules with regard to such sexual conduct. At any rate, probably most peoples of the time regarded it as incongruous that a father and a son should be sexually related to the same woman, even as we would find it incongruous today.

INDICTMENT OF ISRAEL
2:9-16

⁹ "Yet I destroyed the Amorite before them,
  whose height was like the height of the cedars,
  and who was as strong as the oaks;
  I destroyed his fruit above,
    and his roots beneath.
¹⁰ Also I brought you up out of the land of Egypt,
  and led you forty years in the wilderness,
  to possess the land of the Amorite.
¹¹ And I raised up some of your sons for prophets,
  and some of your young men for Nazirites.
  Is it not indeed so, O people of Israel?"

                                          says the Lord.
¹² "But you made the Nazirites drink wine,
  and commanded the prophets,
  saying, 'You shall not prophesy.'
¹³ "Behold, I will press you down in your place,
  as a cart full of sheaves presses down.
¹⁴ Flight shall perish from the swift,
  and the strong shall not retain his strength,
  nor shall the mighty save his life;
¹⁵ he who handles the bow shall not stand,

and he who is swift of foot shall not save himself,
nor shall he who rides the horse save his life;
[16] and he who is stout of heart among the mighty
shall flee away naked in that day,"

says the Lord.

Where the beginning and ending of the preceding
rhetorical unity—if indeed it was ever such a unity—are to
be located, we have no way of telling. Obviously, the
editor of Amos' text, by his reiterated "says the Lord" in
vv 11 and 16 intended that these verses be included in that
unity. Yet we see that they partake of diverse origins.
Thematically they go together, but formally they do not.

We have, first of all, in vv 9-12, what the scholars call a
rîb-prophecy, sometimes called the "prophetic law-suit,"
the most extended instance of which is to be seen in Mic
6:1-8 below. In the *rîb* (which means "litigation") Yahweh
appears not in the guise of judge but rather as plaintiff,
asking for some disinterested jury to judge between him
and the people whom he calls to account.

Yahweh's testimony in his own behalf is manifold. (1)
He rid the promised land of the Amorite aborigines, that
he might prepare it a fit place for the inheritance of his people.
As in the legends of many other peoples, it was thought in
Israel that before it came to be "there were giants in those
days" that by God's power had been replaced. (2) He
liberated his people from their slavery in Egypt and was
with them in their fabled time of wandering in the desert
ere they were brought into this land which had once been
that of the Amorites. Obviously in both these indictments
Amos is tributary to ancient, half-forgotten memories of
the past. So it is with the final charge. (3) He raised up
among this people both "prophets" and "Nazirites." The
two categories evidently were associated in Amos' mind.

Both were—in origin—quite distinct from what prophecy and the nazirite vow (Numbers 6) were in later Israelite times. In origin they were charismatic states related to the "holy warfare" by which Yahweh preserved his people in their initial struggle to possess the land of promise.

The reproach which has been added in v 12 fits in with the *rîb* pattern, but it also looks like a later editorial revision reflecting Israel's experience with prophets and nazirites of times later than those of the conquest of the land. Vv 13-16 are divine threats, assurances in fact, of retribution that inexorably must follow in view of the nation's crimes and its failure to reciprocate the mercies of the Lord. What is being threatened is, obviously, military invasion and conquest—precisely the fate that was to befall Israel at the hands of the New Assyrian Empire another forty years hence.

THE ELECTION OF ISRAEL
3:1-2

> **3** Hear this word that the Lord has spoken against you,
> O people of Israel, against the whole family which I
> brought up out of the land of Egypt:
> ² "You only have I known
> of all the families of the earth;
> therefore I will punish you for all your iniquities.

Over the next several chapters various individual prophecies of Amos, all of which are concerned with God's judgment of his people Israel, have been compiled into a unity. It is not too hard to see how an editor or editors could have done this. On the one hand, there is a series of oracles connected by the recurrent catchphrase "hear this word" which extends from 3:1 to 5:17, followed by another series connected by the catchword "woe" which takes us to the end of chap. 6. In turn, however, these two series which together make up the second part of Amos' prophecy, seem to have been used so as to permit the Lord's word to Israel (and afterwards, when Amos' message was carried to the south, to Judah also) to be heard in two separate emphases. We shall see these in the commentary below.

The section begins with another exordium. "Hear this word that the Lord has spoken against you, O people of Israel." "Against the whole family which I brought up out of the land of Egypt" may very well be a subsequent addition called for by the extension of Amos' prophecies to all of Israel, south as well as north. But the following v 2 is universal in its appeal, whether the charge is lodged against the north or the south or both. What is being said is that Yahweh has chosen Israel out of all the peoples of the earth to be his alone. This choice, "election," must be accounted no glory for the people chosen. Rather, it is the title by which the God of election justifies his punishment—which means devastation—of the land of Israel. He has made his moral will known to this people and therefore has expected from them a degree of conduct not anticipated from the Gentiles. Such is the quixotic favor of a God of grace, whose ways are known to himself alone.

PROPHETIC ASSURANCE
3:3-8

3 "Do two walk together,
  unless they have made an appointment?
4 Does a lion roar in the forest,
  when he has no prey?

> Does a young lion cry out from his den,
>   if he has taken nothing?
> ⁵ Does a bird fall in a snare on the earth,
>   when there is no trap for it?
>   Does a snare spring up from the ground,
>   when it has taken nothing?
> ⁶ Is a trumpet blown in a city,
>   and the people are not afraid?
>   Does evil befall a city,
>   unless the Lord has done it?
> ⁷ Surely the Lord God does nothing,
>   without revealing his secret
>   to his servants the prophets.
> ⁸ The lion has roared;
>   who will not fear?
>   The Lord God has spoken;
>   who can but prophesy?"

These verses form a little redactional unity, the force of which is to insist on the veracity of the prophetic word (Amos') as indicated by homily examples of effect speaking to cause. Amos rests his case on the fact that Yahweh can do and has done to Israel what he will, just as inexorably these conventional signs of the time indicate one thing and nothing else. The precision of v 7 probably is owed, however, to Jer 23:18.

REJECTION OF SAMARIA
3:9-11

> ⁹ Proclaim to the strongholds in Assyria,
>   and to the strongholds in the land of Egypt,
>   and say, "Assemble yourselves upon the mountains
>   of Samaria,

and see the great tumults within her,
and the oppressions in her midst."
¹⁰ "They do not know how to do right,"
says the Lord,
"those who store up violence and robbery
in their strongholds."
¹¹ Therefore thus says the Lord God:
"An adversary shall surround the land,
and bring down your defenses from you,
and your strongholds shall be plundered."

There is no problem with this passage, which sarcastically apostrophizes hated Gentiles (Assyrians in the LXX; Philistines in the Hebrew text) to remark upon the social iniquities that exist within the land of Israel (Samaria). Sardonically, Amos rejoices in the fact that these Gentiles can be aghast at Israel's crimes and therefore understand the inevitable devastation that will befall it.

A REMNANT?
3:12

¹² Thus says the Lord: "As the shepherd rescues from the mouth of the lion two legs, or a piece of an ear, so shall the people of Israel who dwell in Samaria be rescued, with the corner of a couch and parts of a bed."

This is a curious prose passage in the mainly poetic book of Amos. Let us say that, whatever its provenance, it seems to be a parody of the fairly well established postexilic prophetic notion of the "remnant," that is, the faithful few that would survive or had survived the disaster of devastation and (possible) restoration. Yes, says this verse, there will be a remnant—but such a remnant! Scraps and pieces only! For all we know, Amos could have anticipated the idea and ridiculed it in this fashion.

JUDGMENT ON BETHEL
3:13-15

> [13] "Hear, and testify against the house of Jacob,"
>   says the Lord God, the God of hosts,
> [14] "that on the day I punish Israel for his transgressions,
>   I will punish the altars of Bethel,
>   and the horns of the altar shall be cut off
>   and fall to the ground.
> [15] I will smite the winter house with the summer house;
>   and the houses of ivory shall perish,
>   and the great houses shall come to an end,"
>   says the Lord.

This judgment against Bethel may very well have been the one that provoked Amaziah's reaction against Amos as recorded in 7:10. It is the first time in the book of Amos that Bethel has been named—Bethel that was immemorial in Israelite tradition. Bethel that had the most intimate connection with Jacob from whom Israel derived its name and identity (cf. Gen 28:10-22). For a prophet to denounce Bethel, it would seem, would require the effrontery of a devout Roman Catholic proclaiming St. Peter's to be a seedbed of heresy.

If one looks more closely, however, he will see that it is not Bethel primarily that is in Amos' purview, but Bethel merely as it is part of Israel, even symbolic of Israel. Contemporary altars were "horned" at the four corners: whatever may have been the primitive significance of this design, it had come to indicate simply power, just as the horns of a fierce animal were the tokens of its power and strength. Cutting off the horns of Bethel's altar is parallel to the devastation that is cheerfully predicted of Israel's other signs of affluence and careless display of wealth: summer and winter houses, houses of ivory. Unlike Hosea, Amos cares little about the details of Israel's worship. His concern is with the callous display of riches that have been acquired at the cost of human misery.

THE COWS OF BASHAN
4:1-3

4 "Hear this word, you cows of Bashan,
 who are in the mountain of Samaria,
who oppress the poor, who crush the needy,
 who say to their husbands, 'Bring,
  that we may drink!'
² The Lord God has sworn by his holiness
 that, behold, the days are coming upon you,
 when they shall take you away with hooks,
 even the last of you with fishhooks.
³ And you shall go out through the breaches,
 every one straight before her;
 and you shall be cast forth into Harmon,"
            says the Lord.

This passage would seem to confirm what has just been said about the center of Amos' prophetic interest. In recent times various ingenious alternatives have been proposed to the interpretation that has become traditional for these verses. The alternatives have their merit, but the obvious meaning still seems to be the most likely, and it is that which we present here.

Amos is talking about the wealthy matrons of the capital

city of Samaria, the women who above all epitomized the
"establishment" of Israel, not as those who did the actual
moving and shaking of empire but rather as those whose
selfish, thoughtless, insatiable demands made the moving
and shaking of empire inevitable along with the incidental
crushing of the poor over whom their lords had to tread in
order to satisfy their wants. Bashan, at the extreme north-
east of Palestine, was fabled for its lush pastures and,
therefore, for its fat cattle. Amos' characterization of
these women under this term is bitter and sarcastic, but it
also conveys an inescapable truth: it is not the oppressor
alone who is guilty of the oppression, but also he or she
who causes the oppressor to oppress. Hence, Amos willingly tells these women that they will be the first to be led
away into exile when the soon-to-come foreign invasion
brings their little empire crashing down upon their ears.
(The "hooks" mentioned in v 2 are not necessarily a figure
of speech. The Assyrians had a way of leading away cap-
tives by inserting loops into their lips, for example.)

FALSE WORSHIP
4:4-5

> [4] "Come to Bethel, and transgress;
>   to Gilgal, and multiply transgression;
>   bring your sacrifices every morning,
>   your tithes every three days;
> [5] offer a sacrifice of thanksgiving of that
>   which is leavened,
>   and proclaim freewill offerings, publish them;
>   for so you love to do, O people of Israel!"
>
>   says the Lord God.

These verses, in the mind of some commentators, go
with the following not merely as a piece of redaction but in

the original situation of the prophet. This may well be. At the same time, the passage can stand all by itself as Amos' judgment on the worth of cult and liturgy that have no connection with actual life. It is pointless to ask here whether the specifics of the cult ("sacrifices every morning," "tithes every three days," "thanksgiving of that which is leavened," etc.) had any special significance for Amos. He was interested simply in the fact that none of these observances had any real meaning since the spirit of sacrifice which they were supposed to exemplify was in fact completely lacking.

WARNINGS FROM THE PAST
4:6-13

⁶ "I gave you cleanness of teeth in all your cities,
   and lack of bread in all your places,
   yet you did not return to me,"

says the Lord.

⁷ "And I also withheld the rain from you
   when there were yet three months to the harvest;
   I would send rain upon one city,
   and send no rain upon another city;
   one field would be rained upon,
   and the field on which it did not rain withered;

⁸ so two or three cities wandered to one city
   to drink water, and were not satisfied;
   yet you did not return to me,"

says the Lord.

⁹ "I smote you with blight and mildew;
   I laid waste your gardens and your vineyards;
   your fig trees and your olive trees
   the locust devoured;
   yet you did not return to me,"

says the Lord.

¹⁰ "I sent among you a pestilence after the
manner of Egypt;
I slew your young men with the sword;
I carried away your horses;
and I made the stench of your camp
go up into your nostrils;
yet you did not return to me,"

> says the Lord.

¹¹ "I overthrew some of you,
as when God overthrew Sodom and Gomorrah,
and you were as a brand plucked out of the burning;
yet you did not return to me,"

> says the Lord.

¹² "Therefore thus I will do to you, O Israel;
because I will do this to you,
prepare to meet your God, O Israel!"

¹³ For lo, he who forms the mountains,
and creates the wind,
and declares to man what is his thought;
who makes the morning darkness,
and treads on the heights of the earth—
the Lord, the God of hosts, is his name!

In these verses the prophet rehearses various catastrophes which had visited Israel previously and which, in the prophetic purview, were regarded as divinely sent messages of worse things to follow did not the people repent. The persuasion that natural calamities were a sign of divine displeasure endured well into NT times (cf. 1 Cor 11:30) and, as a matter of fact, has never been quite eradicated from the human mind—and, perhaps, should not, if we take the relation of man to his environment altogether seriously. The particular disasters that are recorded here were famine ("cleanness of teeth," v 6), drought (vv 7-8), the burning scirocco wind from Africa combined with a flood of locusts (v 9), some kind of a pestilence (v 10), and, probably, an earthquake (v 11: the earthquake of 1:1?).

It has often been noted that there are frequent correspondences between the evils descibed by Amos and those which are detailed in Leviticus 26, Deuteronomy 28, and 1 Kings 8. In these latter passages we have stylized threats regarding breach of covenant: all these things and others beside shall come upon those who prove to be faithless. The passages probably reflect very ancient traditions of covenantal language. Therefore it is necessary neither to ascribe these present verses to a later editor nor to imagine that Amos, in turn, had been a minister of the official religion, since the language was probably the possession of any contemporary Israelite.

In v 13, however, there is the beginning of a creational hymn that has probably been inserted here by a redactor. The verse makes a fitting doxology to what has gone before, and it will be picked up again in 5:8-9.

LAMENT OVER ISRAEL
5:1-9

5 Hear this word which I take up over you in lamentation, O house of Israel:

[2] "Fallen, no more to rise, is the virgin Israel;
forsaken on her land, with none to raise her up."

[3] For thus says the Lord God:
"The city that went forth a thousand
shall have a hundred left,
and that which went forth a hundred
shall have ten left to the house of Israel."

[4] For thus says the Lord to the house of Israel:
"Seek me and live;

[5] but do not seek Bethel,

> and do not enter into Gilgal
> or cross over to Beer-sheba;
> for Gilgal shall surely go into exile,
> and Bethel shall come to nought."
> [6] Seek the Lord and live,
> lest he break out like fire in the house of Joseph,
> and it devour, with none to quench it for Bethel,
> [7] O you who turn justice to wormwood,
> and cast down righteousness to the earth!
> [8] He who made the Pleiades and Orion,
> and turns deep darkness into the morning,
> and darkens the day into night,
> who calls for the waters of the sea,
> and pours them out upon the surface of the earth,
> the Lord is his name,
> [9] who makes destruction flash forth against the strong,
> so that destruction comes upon the fortress.

These verses are a lament, in which the prophet deplores rather than confidently predicts the coming dissolution of Israel. There is also the note of hope—rare in Amos—the last hope that disaster might be avoided by repentance. "Seek me and live," says Amos, confidently speaking for Yahweh. How is Yahweh to be sought? For the moment, nothing positive is suggested. Where Yahweh is not to be sought, definitely, is in the traditional places of Israel's pilgrimages: Bethel, Gilgal, Beer-sheba. Not because these were bad places—the fact that some are in the north, some in the south of Israel is of no consequence. What was wrong was that they were being sought as a surrogate to true repentance. By "you who turn justice to wormwood, and cast down righteousness to the earth," Amos probably had in mind specifically those who had made a mockery of the courts of law and had converted the rule of justice into an instrument of exploitation. How appropriately comes the redactional doxology in vv 8-9: the Lord, who created all and governs all, will destroy at his will the powerful.

CONDEMNATIONS
5:10-17

> [10] They hate him who reproves in the gate,
>   and they abhor him who speaks the truth.
> [11] Therefore because you trample upon the poor
>   and take from him exactions of wheat,
>   you have built houses of hewn stone,
>   but you shall not dwell in them;
>   you have planted pleasant vineyards,
>   but you shall not drink their wine.
> [12] For I know how many are your transgressions,
>   and how great are your sins—
>   you who afflict the righteous, who take a bribe,
>   and turn aside the needy in the gate.
> [13] Therefore he who is prudent will keep silent
>   in such a time; for it is an evil time.
> [14] Seek good, and not evil,
>   that you may live;
>   and so the Lord, the God of hosts,
>   will be with you, as you have said.
> [15] Hate evil, and love good,
>   and establish justice in the gate;
>   it may be that the Lord, the God of hosts,
>   will be gracious to the remnant of Joseph.
> [16] Therefore thus says the Lord, the God of hosts, the Lord:
>   "In all the squares there shall be wailing;
>   and in all the streets they shall say, 'Alas! alas!'
>   They shall call the farmers to mourning
>   and to wailing those who are skilled in
>   lamentation,

¹⁷ and in all vineyards there shall be wailing,
 for I will pass through the midst of you,"
         says the Lord.

Again we have a mixture of what we can confidently believe were Amos' words along with some others which may be the redaction of his disciples. There is no doubt that all the words are in the spirit of Amos.

The sequence of v 10 with v 7 (skipping over the doxology of vv 8-9) is better appreciated if, with probably the majority of scholars, we take the original wording of v 7 to have been "woe to those. . ." rather than "O you. . ." (the difference in the Hebrew is slight). "They hate him who reproves in the gate" certainly continues the precise thought of v 7. "The gate" in eighth-century Israelite parlance was what "the courts" or "the bench" would mean in our own. It was at the city gate, the forum, meeting place, parliament, and judicature of Israelite society, that justice was handed down—or denied and corrupted. Thus in v 11, the poor from whom are made "exactions of wheat" are undoubtedly the unprotected, the "righteous" of v 12 (read, "the innocent"), who are at the mercy of the powerful who have bought off the establishment to permit the complete exploitation of the poor for whom there are no lobbies, no means of bribery. Those who have thus bled the poor, says Amos, whether at first or at second hand, as agents or as first movers, will never live to enjoy what they thought to have gained by this callous disregard of their fellow Israelites. He was not wrong, even if he did not know when exactly retribution would take place, for take place it was destined to do rather quickly despite the apparent affluence and prosperity of the Israel of Jeroboam II.

The verses that could be redactional are 13-15, where the prophet seems to hold out an easy hope of repentance which could cancel out all of Israel's crimes and allow it to prosper as before. If we look at these verses carefully, however, we recognize that nothing like that is being asserted. "Seek good and not evil" is a cliché: had Israel done such a thing, there would be no need to declare that Yahweh was truly with them as they thought him to be simply in virtue of their self-declared covenant. Only if they should "hate evil, and love good, and (re-)establish justice in the gate," could they have any claim upon the Lord of hosts. And even then, *"it may be "* that Yahweh would have mercy: there is no guarantee. Mercy upon "the remnant of Joseph": if these are indeed Amos' words, he is thinking about a people that already stands in ruins, through self-destruction.

THE DAY OF THE LORD
5:18-27

> [18] Woe to you who desire the day of the Lord!
> Why would you have the day of the Lord?
> It is darkness, and not light;
> [19] as if a man fled from a lion,
> and a bear met him;
> or went into the house and leaned with
> his hand against the wall,
> and a serpent bit him.
> [20] Is not the day of the Lord darkness, and not light,
> and gloom with no brightness in it?
> [21] "I hate, I despise your feasts,
> and I take no delight in your solemn assemblies.
> [22] Even though you offer me your burnt offerings and
> cereal offerings,
> I will not accept them,
> and the peace offerings of your fatted beasts
> I will not look upon.

²³ Take away from me the noise of your songs;
   to the melody of your harps I will not listen.
²⁴ But let justice roll down like waters, and
   righteousness like an everflowing stream.
²⁵"Did you bring to me sacrifices and offerings the
forty years in the wilderness, O house of Israel? ²⁶You
shall take up Sakkuth your king, and Kaiwan your star-
god, your images, which you made for yourselves:
²⁷therefore I will take you into exile beyond Damascus,"
says the Lord, whose name is the God of hosts.

We begin with a bit of Amosian sarcasm. "The day of
the Lord," there seems to be no doubt, was in ancient
Israel the same type of slogan that has been adopted by
later true believers under such titles as "comes the Revolu-
tion," "kommt der Tag," etc. It was thought, in other
words, that on some inevitable day there would be a set-
tling of accounts, when the Lord would intervene to vin-
dicate his own and banish the rest to outer darkness. Yes,
says Amos, such a day is surely coming, but how un-
expected will be its results! Comes *der Tag* and a man con-
gratulates himself to have escaped the lion in the street,
along with the rest of the elect, only to find himself crushed
in a bear-hug. Or he finds refuge breathlessly in a house on
a by-street, leans in relief on the earthen wall, and is bitten
by a serpent! Such is the consolation that Israelites may
take in the expectation of a "Day of the Lord."
    The following vv 21-24 reiterate a view of the cultic wor-
ship of Israel that we have already come to expect of
Amos. It is a complete rejection of Israel's cult, not on any
point of principle but simply because it was the cult of a
hypocritical people. The final v 24 has been variously
taken, and possibly the ambiguity was already inherent in
the verse as it was originally uttered. "Let justice roll down
like waters, and righteousness like an ever-flowing

stream": this can mean, on the one hand, that Israel is being exhorted to substitute justice and righteousness for its meaningless and formalistic rites of sacrifice. It can also mean that the selfsame justice and righteousness will be Yahweh's recompense—in judgment—on a people which has brought him only mouth-honor and no real sacrifice.

The prose vv 25-27 contain ideas that probably exceeded those of Amos, though they did not betray his thought.Did he question the value of sacrifice? In v 25 it is asked whether there were, indeed, sacrifices at all during Israel's formative years. Did he ask whether a God who could be placated by sacrifice without meaning was the true God of Israel? In v 26 alien gods are suggested as those who have been, rather than Yahweh, the object of Israel's worship. It is interesting to note v 27, which determines the Israelites' coming exile as "beyond Damascus." Given the geography of the ancient Near East, Damascus would have been the first port of call for an exile being led out of Palestine. The term "Damascus," however, and probably from this verse of Amos, later became for the Qumran people or for their co-religionists a symbol for the diaspora, for the remnant of the people who would be destined to form the new Israel.

THOSE AT EASE IN SAMARIA
6:1-7

> **6** "Woe to those who are at ease in Zion,
> and to those who feel secure on the mountain
> of Samaria,
> the notable men of the first of the nations,
> to whom the house of Israel come!
> ² Pass over to Calneh, and see;
> and thence go to Hamath the great;

then go down to Gath of the Philistines.
Are they better than these kingdoms?
Or is their territory greater than your territory,
³ O you who put far away the evil day,
and bring near the seat of violence?
⁴ "Woe to those who lie upon beds of ivory,
and stretch themselves upon their couches,
and eat lambs from the flock,
and calves from the midst of the stall;
⁵ who sing idle songs to the sound of the harp,
and like David invent for themselves instruments of
music;
⁶ who drink wine in bowls,
and anoint themselves with the finest oils,
but are not grieved over the ruin of Joseph!
⁷ Therefore they shall now be the first of those to go into
exile,
and the revelry of those who stretch themselves shall
pass away."

If the "woes" of Amos have not been anticipated in 5:7,
they have certainly appeared in 5:18, and now they reap-
pear in v 1, to be taken up again in v 4. "Woe to those who
are at ease in Zion": there is no doubt that that is the way
the prophecy read when it was finally redacted, and rightly
so, since it was properly applied to southern Judah just as
it had first been pronounced against northern Israel. By
the same token, "Zion" doubtless substitutes for an
original northern parallel to Samaria, probably "Bethel."
The prophet asks his auditors, Israelites all, to consider
what little likelihood they have to survive in view of the
fate that has befallen greater nations in the recent past.
Actually, his address, as before, is to the mighty of the
land, the exploiters of the powerless: "the notable men of the

first of the nations [Israel, in virtue of its election], to whom the house of Israel come [for the just dealing that they had the right to expect]." In v 2 the "they" of *RSV* were better rendered "you" (there is no pronoun in the Hebrew, which has to be supplied by the translator), and "is their territory greater than your territory" should read: "was not their territory greater than yours?" The prophet is calling to mind the conquests of various neighboring peoples, possibly at the hands of the Assyrian king Shalmaneser III (858-824 B.C.), though our records are not complete and conquests in the Near East at this time were frequent and routine, so that it is probably impossible to determine just what events were in the mind of the author. The point is that, however minor a figure Calneh, Hamath, and Gath might cut in the annals of world history, all of them doubtless were the political superior of tiny Israel. Hence the ludicrous spectacle of these puny strutters on the little Israelite stage, thinking by their petty shrewdnesses to be able to survive on a policy of business as usual when all the signs of the times were dooming them to inevitable destruction.

In vv 4-7 Amos reverts to the kind of bitter diatribe he poured out on the Bashan cattle of 4:1-3. Beds of ivory, couches of leisure, the choicest of meats, wine, and fine oil—here is the class of privilege, whose sin is not to enjoy the good things of life, but to enjoy them unthinking and unaware of the cost by which they have been purchased by draining the blood of the poor and oppressed. "They are not grieved," he says in amaze, "over the ruin of Joseph." The "ruin of Joseph" refers not to a future but to a present fact: "Joseph," that is to say the people of the north, many of whom claimed descent from the "Joseph" tribes of Ephraim and Manasseh, already lies destroyed by its own will to destroy itself in its social fabric, whatever might be the signs of life that superficially linger on and even give the semblance of prosperity.

CONDEMNATION
6:8

> [8] The Lord God has sworn by himself
> (says the Lord, the God of hosts):
> "I abhor the pride of Jacob,
> and hate his strongholds;
> and I will deliver up the city and all that is in it."

This seems to be an isolated oracle of doom which a redactor has found opportune to insert in this place. Here "Jacob" (= Israel) takes the place of "Joseph," but the message is the same. "The city" could be either Bethel or Samaria, in either case epitomizing Israel. Possibly the most interesting note of the verse is the theological motif of the Lord swearing "by himself." It is an exciting metaphor: God wishes to confirm his purpose by a solemn oath, but of course he can find nothing beyond himself to be the basis of an oath.

THE "REMNANT" AGAIN
6:9-10

> [9] And if ten men remain in one house, they shall die.
> [10]And when a man's kinsman, he who burns him, shall take him up to bring the bones out of the house, and shall say to him who is in the innermost parts of the house, "Is there still any one with you?" he shall say, "No"; and he shall say, "Hush! We must not mention the name of the Lord."

These prose verses may be Amos' or one of his redactors, but there is no question that they reinforce the prophet's previous words about the finality of the promised destruc-

tion of Israel. What is being said is something to this effect: Destruction will be complete, down to the last man.
So much so that when the next of kin, who has the duty of
conducting the proper funerary rites (bringing out the corpse
and burning incense for him) is asked whether there is any
other survivor, he must reply, No!, and superstitiously,
perhaps, avoid mentioning the name of the Lord.

FINAL DESTRUCTION
6:11-14

¹¹ For behold, the Lord commands,
   and the great house shall be smitten into fragments,
   and the little house into bits.
¹² Do horses run upon rocks?
   Does one plow the sea with oxen?
   But you have turned justice into poison
   and the fruit of righteousness into wormwood—
¹³ you who rejoice in Lo-debar, who say,
   "Have we not by our own strength
   taken Karnaim for ourselves?"
¹⁴ "For behold, I will raise up against you a nation,
   O house of Israel," says the Lord, the God of hosts;
   "and they shall oppress you from the entrance of
   Hamath
   to the Brook of the Arabah."

These are the last words in this section in which Amos
predicts absolute destruction for Israel. There is an interesting development in v 12, in that the prophet indicates
that there is a law in nature itself which points to what is
right and what is wrong. Do you ride horses over rocks?
Obviously not. Do you plow the sea with oxen? Of course
not. What is the difference, however, when you "turn"
justice into poison and the fruit of righteousness into

wormwood—we are reminded that this "turn" is a juridical term, equivalent to saying that the provisions of due
process have been aborted. Amos states that the frustra-
tion of elementary justice is, in other word, not only an of-
fence to the Almighty but also the violation of a law of observed nature.

The Lo-debar and Karnaim of v 13 look like place names:
probably the sites of battles wherein Israel had been victor-
ious over its enemies and which, therefore, had become
popular slogans of future invincibility. Not so, says the
Lord. Israel shall be overrun from north to south by a foe
whom its God himself will send against them in retribution.

VISIONS
7:1-9

7 Thus the Lord God showed me: behold, he was
forming locusts in the beginning of the shooting up of
the latter growth; and lo, it was the latter growth after
the king's mowings.

²When they had finished eating the grass of the land, I
said,

"O Lord God, forgive, I beseech thee!

How can Jacob stand?

He is so small!"

³ The Lord repented concerning this;

"It shall not be," said the Lord.

⁴ Thus the Lord God showed me: behold, the Lord God
was calling for a judgment by fire, and it devoured the
great deep and was eating up the land.

⁵ Then I said,

"O Lord God, cease, I beseech thee!

How can Jacob stand?

He is so small!"

⁶ The Lord repented concerning this;

"This also shall not be," said the Lord God.

⁷ He showed me: behold, the Lord was standing beside
a wall built with a plumb line, with a plumb line in his
hand. ⁸And the Lord said to me, "Amos, what do you
see?" And I said, "A plumb line." Then the Lord said,

"Behold, I am setting a plumb line in the midst of my
people Israel;

I will never again pass by them;

⁹ the high places of Isaac shall be made desolate,
and the sanctuaries of Israel shall be laid waste,
and I will rise against the house of
Jeroboam with the sword."

There follow three visions (a fourth will appear in 8:1-3
and a fifth in 9:1), a series of revelations given to the prophet not simply by a "word" which he announces but by a
"word" that he professes to have discerned in some
specified occurrence. Several things are to be noted. First
of all, the "vision" seems to be, at least in the usual case,
simply a normal observance on the part of the prophet in
which he sees some revealed significance. Secondly, there
is a distinct and repetitive formula adopted in the recountal
of the vision which can only speak to a conventional
literary form that had been adopted to describe it. And
finally, at least in the first two visions, the prophet appears
in the unusual posture of a pleader for Israel, appealing to
the Lord and actually securing from him the assurance that
the promised devastation would not actually occur.

First, the vision of the locusts. A locust swarm ruining a
crop was hardly unheard of in Palestine. "The king's
mowing" would presumably have been the better, earlier
growth, owed to the feudal lord. Now come the locusts.
Though Amos does not say so explicitly, the sense is clear:
the coming of the locusts now upon the land signifies the
total destruction that is threatened to Israel. Yet this once,

Amos intercedes, and the Lord withdraws his anger.

Instead of a "judgment by fire" in v 4 (which makes little sense either visually or grammatically), "a rain of fire" is the better translation. What Amos is probably talking about is a great drought, the burning wind and heat which descend upon Palestine from heaven and dry up its water supplies. Once again, having seen this terrible visitation, Amos intercedes successfully with the Lord.

Thirdly, the vision of *anak*. "Plumb line" (derived from the notion that the Hebrew word means "lead" and that a plumb line or plummet of lead was a traditional symbol of a nation being measured for destruction, cf. 2 Kgs 21:13) is the conventional translation of this word. We do not know, however, whether this rendering is correct at all. All that we do know is that Amos again undoubtedly saw some conventional object to which he attached a revelatory significance from the Lord. This time there is no intercession on his part: destruction is inevitable. The "high places" (in Deuteronomic language, places of illicit worship) and "sanctuaries" (according to Deuteronomy, only one sanctuary was lawful) probably have no special significance for Amos; along with "the house of Jeroboam," they indicate to him simply the symbols of the Israelite establishment.

A BIOGRAPHICAL INTERLUDE
7:10-17

[10] Then Amaziah the priest of Bethel sent to Jeroboam king of Israel, saying, "Amos has conspired against you in the midst of the house of Israel; the land is not able to bear all his words. [11] For thus Amos has said,

'Jeroboam shall die by the sword,
and Israel must go into exile away from his land.' "

¹² And Amaziah said to Amos, "O seer, go, flee away to the land of Judah, and eat bread there, and prophesy there; ¹³but never again prophesy at Bethel, for it is the king's sanctuary, and it is a temple of the kingdom."
¹⁴ Then Amos answered Amaziah, "I am no prophet, nor a prophet's son; but I am a herdsman, and a dresser of sycamore trees, ¹⁵and the Lord took me from following the flock, and the Lord said to me, 'Go, prophesy to my people Israel.'
¹⁶ "Now therefore hear the word of the Lord.
You say, 'Do not prophesy against Israel,
and do not preach against the house of Isaac.'
¹⁷ Therefore thus says the Lord:
'Your wife shall be a harlot in the city,
and your sons and your daughters
shall fall by the sword,
and your land shall be parceled out by line;
you yourself shall die in an unclean land,
and Israel shall surely go into exile
away from its land.' "

"The house of Jeroboam," in any case, in the preceding vision explains the insertion at this point of the biographical passage—doubtless remembered by Amos' disciples—that now appears.

Amaziah, the priest of Bethel, was certainly the cultic person in charge of this royal sanctuary, the sanctuary into which Amos had intruded. From Amaziah's standpoint, here was an interloper violating all the rules of hierarchical procedure. He cannot be faulted for having summed up for Jeroboam the true threat that Amos seemed to present, as a radical agitator who was disturbing the good order of the peaceful and imperial realm of Jeroboam II.

Therefore he exhorted Amos to get himself back to Judah, to make his living there by his prophecy, and to disturb no longer the tranquility of Bethel.

It was probably this last assumption of Amaziah, the assumption that Amos was like the other prophets with whom he was familiar and many of whom were in his stable for comfortable prophecies, that prompted Amos' famous statement in v 14:

"I am no prophet,
　　nor a prophet's son,"

said Amos in reply. He used the only language that Amaziah would understand. Amaziah thought of him in conventional terms, of prophets who were in the hire of courts, sanctuaries, and the like, prophets for favorable oracles, who could be dismissed at will for their defects.

"I am a herdsman and a dresser of sycamore trees,
　　and the Lord took me from following the flock,
and the Lord said to me,
　　'Go, prophesy to my people Israel.'"

Amos tells Amaziah that he has totally misunderstood Amos, who is not one of his hirelings but a charismatic of the Lord. Correspondingly, vv 16-17 are not, as they have often been thought to be, some kind of vindictive verdict that the prophet uttered over an adversary. All that they encompass, really, is an inclusion of Amaziah in the general condemnation that Amos has already indicated to be the fate of Israel.

THE VISION OF THE FRUIT
8:1-14

> **8** Thus the Lord God showed me: behold, a basket of summer fruit. ²And he said, "Amos, what do you see?" And I said, "A basket of summer fruit." Then the Lord said to me,
> 　　"The end has come upon my people Israel;

I will never again pass by them.
³ The songs of the temple shall become wailings in that day,"

                           says the Lord God;
   "the dead bodies shall be many;
   in every place they shall be cast out in silence."
⁴ Hear this, you who trample upon the needy,
   and bring the poor of the land to an end,
⁵ saying, "When will the new moon be over,
   that we may sell grain?
   And the sabbath,
   that we may offer wheat for sale,
   that we may make the ephah small and the shekel great,
   and deal deceitfully with false balances,
⁶ that we may buy the poor for silver
   and the needy for a pair of sandals,
   and sell the refuse of the wheat?"
⁷ The Lord has sworn by the pride of Jacob:
   "Surely I will never forget any of their deeds.
⁸ Shall not the land tremble on this account,
   and every one mourn who dwells in it,
   and all of it rise like the Nile,
   and be tossed about and sink again,
   like the Nile of Egypt?"
⁹ "And on that day," says the Lord God,
   "I will make the sun go down at noon,
   and darken the earth in broad daylight.
¹⁰ I will turn your feasts into mourning,
   and all your songs into lamentation;
   I will bring sackcloth upon all loins,
   and baldness on every head;
   I will make it like the mourning for an only son,
   and the end of it like a bitter day.
¹¹ "Behold, the days are coming," says the Lord God,

"when I will send a famine on the land;
not a famine of bread, nor a thirst for water,
but of hearing the words of the Lord.
[12] They shall wander from sea to sea,
and from north to east;
they shall run to and fro, to seek the word of the
Lord,
but they shall not find it.
[13] "In that day the fair virgins and the young men
shall faint for thirst.
[14] Those who swear by Ashimah of Samaria,
and say, 'As thy god lives, O Dan,'
and, 'As the way of Beer-sheba lives,'
they shall fall, and never rise again."

The chapter begins in vv 1-3 with another vision, inter-rupted in 7:10-17 preceding, by the biographical section. Here again is a typical prophetic "vision," a look at sum-mer (*qayits*) fruit, fruit that is overripe, which suggests that the end (*qets*) of Israel is coming.

Attached to this vision are the rest of the verses of this chapter which belong more properly with oracles that have occurred before, concerning Amos' quarrel with the high and mighty of Israel. It is doubtful if there is any necessity to comment further than has already been observed. The sole exception, perhaps, is to note that, from whatever time, v 8 looks like the recollection of an earthquake, and v 9 like an eclipse of the sun. The other verses are fairly routine.

VISION OF THE ALTAR
9:1

9 I saw the Lord standing beside the altar, and he said:

"Smite the capitals until the thresholds shake,
and shatter them on the heads of all the people;
and what are left of them I will slay with the sword;
not one of them shall flee away,
not one of them shall escape.

When we get into this last chapter of the book of Amos
we sense that we grow increasingly more remote from the
eighth-century prophet whose voice we have been hearing
in however diluted form in the previous chapters. Take this
final "vision," for example. If it is a vision of Amos, it dif-
fers markedly from the earlier visions in which there is a
routine observance to which a word of prophetic insight
has been attached. We do not know what to make about a
vision of the Lord standing "by the altar," unless we conclude, as we suspect, that this is a contrived vision in imitation of what has gone before in order to condemn the sanctuary of Bethel, in Judahite eyes *ipso facto* a place of
unlawful worship, though for Amos it had been merely a
place where unlawful people worshipped.

A HYMN
9:2-6

2 "Though they dig into Sheol,
   from there shall my hand take them;
   though they climb up to heaven,
   from there I will bring them down.
3 Though they hide themselves on the top of Carmel,
   from there I will search out and take them;
   and though they hide from my sight
   at the bottom of the sea,
   there I will command the serpent,
   and it shall bite them.

⁴ And though they go into captivity before
their enemies,
there I will command the sword, and
it shall slay them;
and I will set my eyes upon them
for evil and not for good."
⁵ The Lord, God of hosts,
he who touches the earth and it melts
and all who dwell in it mourn,
and all of it rises like the Nile,
and sinks again, like the Nile of Egypt;
⁶ who builds his upper chambers in the heavens,
and founds his vault upon the earth;
who calls for the waters of the sea,
and pours them out upon the surface
of the earth—
the Lord is his name.

See the comment below 4:13,5:8-9. All of these verses
seem to belong to the same hymn touching on the powers
of Yahweh. It has frequently been called a creational
hymn, and such it is in large part. But it also involves an as-
pect of Yahweh that has nothing to do necessarily with
creation but simply celebrates his dominance. Whether we
conceive the passage to have been adapted by Amos to his
purposes or to have been appended by an editor sympathe-
tic to Amos' purposes, the message is the same. This is a
God whose control is universal, whose retribution no one
can escape: there is no area known to man or woman,
above, below, beneath, or in the farthest regions, into
which his power does not extend. There is no escape for the
wicked.

THE LORD CASTS OFF HIS PEOPLE
9:7-10

> [7] "Are you not like the Ethiopians to me,
>   O people of Israel?" says the Lord.
>   "Did I not bring up Israel from the
>   land of Egypt,
>   and the Philistines from Caphtor
>   and the Syrians from Kir?
> [8] Behold, the eyes of the Lord God are upon the sinful
>   kingdom,
>   and I will destroy it from the surface of the ground;
>   except that I will not utterly destroy the house of
>   Jacob,"
>   says the Lord.
> [9] "For lo, I will command,
>   and shake the house of Israel among all the nations
>   as one shakes with a sieve,
>   but no pebble shall fall upon the earth.
> [10] All the sinners of my people shall die by the sword,
>   who say, 'Evil shall not overtake or meet us.' "

These verses do begin to sound like Amos again. The touch of authenticity is contributed by the peoples whom Amos has chosen to set alongside Israel as equally worthy of divine attention: Kush (of unknown origin), Philistia (from Caphtor), and Aram (from Kir). Nondescript nations. If we are to interpret Amos for what he in all probability said, he ended by repudiating Yahweh's election of Israel, saying that they were of no more concern to him than the Gentiles beyond the pale. This is perfectly in keeping with Amos' view of God's judgment as we have seen it so far. Israel had forfeited its every right to divine protection and now, therefore, must subside into the silence of history that had been decreed for a thousand other nations that had preceded it and would succeed it. For Amos, Israel was finished.

CONCLUSION
9:11-15

[11] "In that day I will raise up
the booth of David that is fallen
and repair its breaches, and raise up its ruins,
and rebuild it as in the days of old;
[12] that they may possess the remnant of Edom
and all the nations who are called by my name,"
says the Lord who does this.
[13] "Behold, the days are coming," says the Lord,
"when the plowman shall overtake the reaper
and the treader of grapes him who sows the seed;
the mountains shall drip sweet wine,
and all the hills shall flow with it.
[14] I will restore the fortunes of my people Israel,
and they shall rebuild the ruined cities and inhabit them;
they shall plant vineyards and drink their wine,
and they shall make gardens and eat their fruit.
[15] I will plant them upon their land,
and they shall never again be plucked up
out of the land which I have given them,"
says the Lord your God.

What, then, are we to make of these final verses, in which a glorious future is predicted of the coming Israel? First of all, the Israel that is envisaged is not that of the eighth-century prophet Amos, for whom it was the Northern Kingdom, but rather a united (and ideal) Israel which would be the result of Judah and Israel (the latter had ceased to exist) coming together again in a single kingdom with the expectation of a same Davidic king. This construct is postexilic romanticism, and the picture that is presented here is idyllic. Nothing remotely resembling the myth ever really happened, and therefore there is no point on commenting on the verses historically. They are the work of a visionary whose idea of the ultimate purposes of the Lord quite transcends everything that the Old Testament was able to accomplish.

HOSEA

THE TITLE
1:1

1 The word of the Lord that came to Hosea the son of Beeri, in the days of Uzziah, Jotham, Ahaz, and Hezekiah, kings of Judah, and in the days of Jeroboam the son of Joash, king of Israel.

THE TITLE, as usual, seeks to identify the prophet in terms of the reigning Judahite kings who were contemporary with the kings in Israel. Uzziah (783-742 B.C.), Jotham (742-735), Ahaz (735-715), and Hezekiah (715-687) probably accurately locate the prophet in time as does the note that he flourished in the reign of Jeroboam (II) of Israel (786-746). Hosea was a younger contemporary of Amos, the main difference between the two being that while Amos was a southern interloper into Israel, Hosea was a native of the land and therefore had a more proprietary right to speak in its condemnation or in its defense.

THE PROPHET'S MARRIAGE
1:2-9

² When the Lord first spoke through Hosea, the Lord said to Hosea, "Go, take to yourself a wife of harlotry

and have children of harlotry, for the land commits great harlotry by forsaking the Lord." ³So he went and took Gomer the daughter of Diblaim, and she conceived and bore him a son.

⁴ And the Lord said to him, "Call his name Jezreel; for yet a little while, and I will punish the house of Jehu for the blood of Jezreel, and I will put an end to the kingdom of the house of Israel. ⁵And on that day, I will break the bow of Israel in the valley of Jezreel."

⁶ She conceived again and bore a daughter. And the Lord said to him, "Call her name Not pitied, for I will no more have pity on the house of Israel, to forgive them at all. ⁷But I will have pity on the house of Judah, and I will deliver them by the Lord their God; I will not deliver them by bow, nor by sword, nor by war, nor by horses, nor by horsemen."

⁸ When she had weaned Not pitied, she conceived and bore a son. ⁹And the Lord said, "Call his name Not my people, for you are not my people and I am not your God."

"When the Lord first spoke to Hosea, the Lord said to Hosea, etc." It should be noted that the Lord's *word* to Hosea is, first and foremost, a command for him to *do* something, which is in turn a requirement that he do a rather extraordinary thing, that is prophesy for his people. "Take to yourself a wife of harlotry." Was the prophet being asked to take to his bosom a known whore, or is the sense subtler: Hosea married a Gomer who eventually proved herself to be a faithless spouse, even as Israel did? It is impossible to decide. In any case, whether symbolically or in fact (and the latter is more likely in virtue of the rest of the prophecy), Hosea marries himself to a faithless woman who represents to him as a prophetic word of the Lord the faithlessness of Israel towards Yahweh who had taken it to himself in marriage by way of the covenant.

The children produced by the union of Hosea and Gomer all have symbolic names (cf. the similar Shear-jashub of Isa 7:3 and the Maher-shalal-hash-baz of Isa 8:1-4). Whether these were names in fact or have been invented for the purpose of the prophetic narrative, depends on the character of Hosea's marital experience from the standpoint of history: where its actual existence leaves off and its prophetic symbolism begins. In any case, the names of the second and third children are quite obvious: "Not my people" and "Not pitied" (better, "not loved" with the love that is owed in the covenant relationship); Yahweh is about to cast off his faithless spouse Israel.

The name of the first of Hosea's children needs some explanation. It was in the valley of Jezreel, a proverbial battleground in Palestine, that Jehu had put to a bloody end the dynasty of Omri and had replaced it by his own, now represented in the reigning monarch Jeroboam II (cf. 2 Kings 9-10). Now the Lord is about to put an end to this dynasty, repaying it for all the evils over which it has presided, epitomizing as it did all that was wrong with Israel. Hence, "Jezreel" is as much a name of doom as is "Not pitied" or "Not my people."

It is interesting to contrast the narrative of 2 Kings 9-10, by one who was a prophetical author of sorts and who rather approved of Jehu's bloody deeds in the name of the Lord, with the censorious and condemnatory view taken by the book of Hosea. The contrast has something to say with regard to relative proximity to the events and what subsequent history had shown, but also, perhaps, with regard to the variety of prophetic interpretation of Israel's experience with God.

FINAL SALVATION
1:10-2:1

> [10] Yet the number of the people of Israel shall be like the sand of the sea, which can be neither measured nor

numbered; and in the place where it was said to them,
"You are not my people," it shall be said to them,
"Sons of the living God." ¹¹And the people of Judah
and the people of Israel shall be gathered together, and
they shall appoint for themselves one head; and they
shall go up from the land, for great shall be the day of
Jezreel.

2 Say to your brother, "My people," and to your
sister, "She has obtained pity."

These three verses (which are 2:1-3 in the Hebrew text
and in the *New American Bible*) have been anticipated by
1:7 above, where it was stated that the doom awaiting
Israel would not, eventually, overcome Judah but rather
that it would be delivered by God's mercy. All these verses
are the work of a prophetic hand considerably later than
Hosea's, a hand that used Hosean language and was trying
thereby to adjust its message to altered times and conditions. It will be noted that now "Jezreel" has become once
more a symbol of salvation and triumph, as it so often was
in the long history of Israel's battles.

The verses date, obviously, from a time when the northern Israel where Hosea had prophesied was no more (its
definitive dissolution occurred with the fall of Samaria in
721 B.C.) and only the southern Judah remained. This is
only one of the several instances in the book of Hosea
where it becomes apparent that the prophet's message retained significance for another, comparable audience once
its original one had ceased to exist. But it is possible to pin-
point the date of these prophecies more precisely than
simply post-721 B.C., when Hosea's words were brought
south and applied to Judah. For Judah, too, it is evident
from these verses, has fallen prey to disaster and is in need
of redemption. By the power of God, says the prophet of
these verses, Judah will be delivered, and not only that:

Israel and Judah shall be reunited into a single kingdom and the old covenant terms shall be restored—"children of God," "my people ."

The prophecy of a restored and reunited Israel and Judah was a favored theme of the exilic age (after 597 B.C.) and particularly of the exilic prophet Ezekiel (cf. Ezek 37:15-22, for example). The prophecy was never actually to be fulfilled; history thwarted it. Intransigence on the part of both the Judahites who returned to Jerusalem after their Babylonian captivity and of the Israelites and Judahites who had remained in the land over the period of captivity produced separate and irreconcilable societies that were never able to reunite (see the books of Ezra and Nehemiah). Out of the exile emerged a more or less rigid Judaism represented in most of the later books of the canonical Old Testament like Joel or Obadiah, the kind of Judaism that produced the Pharisaism of the New Testament. Alongside it survived the "heterodox" "people of the land" which knew nothing of the law, the *torah,* that had been elaborated in captivity as the ultimate revelation of God (cf. John 7:49). Alongside, too, were those who on more doctrinaire grounds stood for the "old religion," in some sense the predecessors of the Sadducees of the New Testament; at the same time there could be found the dissenters from "orthodox" Judaism in basic matters, represented variously in works like Sirach, Ruth, and Jonah. Alongside, finally, were the Samaritans, basically the descendants of the Israelites of the north, who by New Testament times constituted a religion and separate tradition which both they and the Jews recognized to be hostile to Judaism as Judaism was hostile to Samaritanism (John 4:7-9; that the Good Samaritan was, indeed, good is, of course, the paradoxical point of Jesus' parable in Lk 10:29-37).

The contrast between what prophecy envisioned and what

in fact did eventually take place is frequent in the Bible.
That the prophecy was not, in fact, actualized in the subsequent flow of events, constitutes no argument against the
validity of the prophecy. Prophecy expressed the will and
plan of God, which always was and is capable of being temporarily frustrated by the machinations of man.

REPUDIATION OF FAITHLESS ISRAEL
2:2-15

> [2] "Plead with your mother, plead—
> for she is not my wife, and I am not her husband—
> that she put away her harlotry from her face,
> and her adultery from between her breasts;
> [3] lest I strip her naked
> and make her as in the day she was born,
> and make her like a wilderness,
> and set her like a parched land,
> and slay her with thirst.
> [4] Upon her children also I will have no pity,
> because they are children of harlotry.
> [5] For their mother has played the harlot;
> she that conceived them has acted shamefully.
> For she said, 'I will go after my lovers,
> who give me my bread and my water,
> my wool and my flax, my oil and my drink.'
> [6] Therefore I will hedge up her way with thorns;
> and I will build a wall against her,
> so that she cannot find her paths.
> [7] She shall pursue her lovers,
> but not overtake them;
> and she shall seek them,
> but shall not find them.
> Then she shall say, 'I will go
> and return to my first husband,
> for it was better with me then than now.'

⁸ And she did not know
   that it was I who gave her
   the grain, the wine, and the oil,
   and who lavished upon her silver
   and gold which they used for Baal.
⁹ Therefore I will take back
   my grain in its time,
   and my wine in its season;
   and I will take away my wool and my flax,
   which were to cover her nakedness.
¹⁰ Now I will uncover her lewdness
   in the sight of her lovers,
   and no one shall rescue her out of my hand.
¹¹ And I will put an end to all her mirth,
   her feasts, her new moons, her sabbaths,
   and all her appointed feasts.
¹² And I will lay waste her vines and her fig trees,
   of which she said,
   'These are my hire,
   which my lovers have given me.'
   I will make them a forest,
   and the beasts of the field shall devour them.
¹³ And I will punish her for the feast days of the Baals
   when she burned incense to them
   and decked herself with her ring and jewelry,
   and went after her lovers,
   and forgot me, says the Lord.
¹⁴ "Therefore, behold, I will allure her,
   and bring her into the wilderness,
   and speak tenderly to her.
¹⁵ And there I will give her her vineyards,
   and make the Valley of Achor a door of hope.
   And there she shall answer as in the days of her
   youth,
   as at the time when she came out of the land of Egypt.

These are vv 4-17 in the Hebrew text and in the *New American Bible*.

From chap. l, which is biographical, there appears to be in chap. 2 a probably autobiographical section which in chap. 3 becomes certainly autobiographical. These three chapters of Hosea are obviously distinct from the accumulation of prophecies that follow them. They are, without question, as is true of chap. 7 of Amos, the work of Hoseanic disciples who have prefaced to the words of their master the record of experiences that were formative of his thought and that had produced the prophecy for which he was remembered.

First of all, Hosea divorces his wife: "She is not my wife, and I am not her husband." So simple was the divorce process in ancient Israel, and so simply has Yahweh cast off the people that he had acquired to himself at such expense. The details are distasteful. That an adulterous woman should be shamed by being stripped naked before her own children was a terrible thing. In these verses allegory and the allegorized become mingled, sometimes confusedly. On the one hand the people—obviously, that part of the people, still of good will, to whom Hosea can make his appeal—are exhorted to plead (the term is a juridical one) in favor of their mother that the shameful divorce process be not necessary. At the same time it is recognized that the plan will be without avail, that Israel is indeed guilty as charged. She has preferred to Yahweh "her lovers," and therefore she is an adulteress. The "lovers," as the subsequent verses leave us in no doubt, were for Hosea the indigenous gods of Canaan, the deities of the "old" religion, a religion alien to that of Yahwism whose historical ethos was an import into Canaan. Unlike Amos, who showed little concern about religious forms and practices, Hosea more perceptively recognized the principle that rite and ritual were an index to what people really believed and to what they did in consequence of what they believed. Hosea no less than Amos was far more interested in mercy and justice than he was in the proprieties of sacrifice, but he was better than Amos at seeing what was the connection between the two.

The allegory continues. Now (v 4) "her children" are obviously to be identified with Gomer herself, the nation to be cast off. Why? Because they have put their trust in the gods of the land rather than in the Yahweh of their historical experience. To translate the text into contemporary terms: idolatry is to worship the person or national ego—admittedly a manifestation of the divine in many ways—in preference to the notion of a God who sits above national and racial boundaries and dispenses his justice without regard to any privilege. The God of Israel is no more bound to Bethel, Mizpah, or Ephraim, than is the God of American civil religion constrained to defend a short-lived American Republic against the forces from without that would challenge its native resources of innate virtue and vigor.

Unlike Amos, Hosea is compassionate. Hosea will divorce his wife—Yahweh will divorce his people—not for destruction but for redemption. The punishments which will descend upon Israel are in Hosea no less certain than they are in Amos, but they are directed towards renovation and not simply to destruction. This is the message of vv 7-15: by means of the sorrows that will inevitably fall upon Israel, Israel will be brought to the realization that trust in the gods of Canaan has been illusory. They have profited nothing. Yahweh alone, the God of Israel's historical experience, has been responsible for whatever prosperity it has enjoyed. The withdrawal of his protection which Hosea now proclaims will be the proof of this claim. What Israel must now do—and what Hosea confidently believes will happen—is that it recognize these facts, return to its primitive faith, and eschew the idolatry of its self-worship which was to identify its interests with the gods of the land.

THE NEW COVENANT
2:16-23

[16] "And in that day, says the Lord, you will call me, 'My husband,' and no longer will you call me, 'My Baal.' [17]For I will remove the names of the Baals from her mouth, and they shall be mentioned by name no more. [18]And I will make for you a covenant on that day with the beasts of the field, the birds of the air, and the creeping things of the ground; and I will abolish the bow, the sword, and war from the land; and I will make you lie down in safety. [19]And I will betroth you to me for ever; I will betroth you to me in righteousness and in justice, in steadfast love, and in mercy. [20]I will betroth you to me in faithfulness; and you shall know the Lord.
[21] "And in that day, says the Lord,
  I will answer the heavens
  and they shall answer the earth;
[22]and the earth shall answer the grain,
  the wine, and the oil,
  and they shall answer Jezreel;
[23] and I will sow him for myself in the land.
  And I will have pity on Not pitied,
  and I will say to Not my people,
  'You are my people';
  and he shall say, 'Thou art my God.' "

These are vv 18-25 in the Hebrew and in the *New American Bible*.

At first glance, these verses seem to follow quite easily from the preceding. On closer examination, however, it becomes apparent that the tone has changed pronouncedly. No longer is there question of a God who punishes in order to redeem. Rather, redemption is here promised free, as a pure gift without prior condition. The tone is that of Jeremiah 31, a consolation to a people that has paid its dues in suffering and now will be restored. Most scholars are in agreement that the prophet Jeremiah is dependent upon his predecessor Hosea and has borrowed ideas from him. In this present instance, there is some suspicion that a Hosean redactor has repaid the debt by introducing Jeremian ideas into this passage of Hosea. Whatever is to be said of the ultimate authorship of these verses, in any case, there is no doubt that they encapsulate in very few words a thoroughgoing biblical theology of covenant. First of all there is a play on words. No longer, says the prophet, will Israel address its god/husband as Baal (=the name of the god of Canaan, but also="lord," "master," the subservient title by which an Israelite wife knew her husband). Rather, her God will be "her man" ("husband" in the text above), corresponding to a more humane conception of the marital relationship. Secondly, God's reconciliation with man will entail a restoration of the universe to its primitive harmony as intended by God (v 18): the world that was put in disorder because of human transgression (Gen 3:17-19) will be restored as it should have been. And finally, a galaxy of covenantal theological words is gathered together in vv 19-20.

"I will betroth you," says the Lord. In Near Eastern terms, this signifies the bridal gift which the husband bestows upon his bride. The bride here is Israel, and the betrothal gift is "for ever." It consists in "righteousness" *(ṣedeq),* in "justice" *(mishpaṭ),* in "steadfast love" *(ḥesed),* and in "mercy" *(raḥamim).* We are using the Hebrew words here alongside the conventional translations not to suggest that the latter are incorrect, but simply to assert, as no one will deny, that they are perforce inadequate. They are inadequate simply because no single sentence can sum up centuries of religious experience. Together they make up what is practically a distilled vocabulary of prophetic theology as regards the relation of God to his people. What he will do, if we take the verses at face value, is to endow the people of his choice with his own attributes. An astounding act of grace!—hardly to be exceeded by anything in the New Testament promising redemption for the repentant sinner.

Once again, we note (in v 22), "Jezreel" has taken on a salvific meaning, in keeping with the reversal in these verses of the lot of "Not pitied" and "Not my people."

THE FAITHLESS WIFE REDEEMED
3:1-5

> **3** And the Lord said to me, "Go again, love a woman who is beloved of a paramour and is an adulteress; even as the Lord loves the people of Israel, though they turn to other gods and love cakes of raisins." ²So I bought her for fifteen shekels of silver and a homer and a lethech of barley. ³And I said to her, "You must dwell as mine for many days; you shall not play the harlot, or belong to another man; so will I also be to you." ⁴For the children of Israel shall dwell many days without king or prince, without sacrifice or pillar, without ephod or teraphim. ⁵Afterward the children of Israel shall return and seek the Lord their God, and David their king; and they shall come in fear to the Lord and to his goodness in the latter days.

In chap. 1 we had biography; now we have autobiography. The point can be made whether the "again" of v 1 refers to a new experience in the prophet's life or rather to a resumption of an old experience—whether he is being told to take yet another adulterous and harlot woman to wife or rather to ransom back to his bed the faithless Gomer who had deserted him. We think we are in the company of most interpreters of the text when we decide that it is, indeed, Gomer that is in its purview. Hosea— prophetically playing the part of the God of Israel— recalls his faithless wife and makes it possible for her to become that for which she was originally designed. It is to be noted that the action is entirely on the part of Hosea (= God) and not on the merits or even repentance of Gomer (= Israel). We are dealing in other words, with an act of complete divine grace, dispensed gratuitously without prior claim and for no reason other than the divine beneficence.

Gomer had merited a sentence of death (Deut 22:22, Lev 20:10): that was the law. But God (Hosea) will not be bound by law, not even his own law. He will show mercy, or gospel, that extends beyond law. For law is what regulates the affairs of men according to the ordinarily sensible rules that men have devised to regulate their polities. Grace is a vastly different thing.

To be brief, what this text says is that (in principle) Israel has been redeemed: the Lord has (in principle) bought it back, reacquired it. Whatever the details of silver shekels and barley measures may be as they enter into the ransom price, they have little to do with the prophet's message. They merely add a concrete dimension to the symbolism by which Hosea's experience with Gomer continues to represent Yahweh's with Israel. For the moment, though the eventual salvation of Israel is implied, we are left explicitly only with its possibility, following on the medicinal experience of an exile which lies ahead. That is what v 4 is all about: paradoxically, Yahweh's redemption of Israel is, first of all, the deprivation of his presence with Israel. Grace is mercy and it is dispensed freely, but it must not be confused with simple-minded benignity unconcerned with justice. Hosea does not take Gomer back without conditions. Israel must suffer the loss of the national and religious tokens of her identity in order to learn how little this identity had been prized and with what justice it had been taken from her.

The final verse of this chapter, with its talk of "the latter days" and its evocation of the Davidic messianic king, seems to be a later amplification of the text reflecting exilic and postexilic salvation thinking when once again "Israel" meant the whole united people of God (see above on 1:10-2:1).

THE CASE AGAINST ISRAEL
4:1-3

4 Hear the word of the Lord, O people of Israel;
for the Lord has a controversy
with the inhabitants of the land.
There is no faithfulness or kindness,
and no knowledge of God in the land;
² there is swearing, lying, killing, stealing, and committing adultery;
they break all bounds and murder follows murder.
³ Therefore the land mourns,
and all who dwell in it languish,
and also the beasts of the field,
and the birds of the air;
and even the fish of the sea are taken away.

We now begin the second part of the prophecy of

Hosea, which extends all the way to the end of the book. As quickly becomes evident, this part consists of many individual prophecies, usually relatively brief, which have simply been gathered together and allowed to speak for themselves. Many attempts have been made by authors to discern the order or rationale that was in the mind of the compiler in accordance with which he distributed the prophetic units which were in his possession, but none of these has won general acceptance. The best we can do is consider each prophecy as it comes in the text.

The first begins as a *rîb,* a prophetic "lawsuit," in which Israel is summoned to the bar of justice to answer to the case against it. The theme in this instance, however, is merely a device to indict Israel in radical and generic terms rather than to enter into specific crimes. For that reason these verses quite aptly introduce Hosea's collected prophecy, incorporating as they do what may be called the basic theology underlying his condemnation of the specifics that will be mentioned in later verses.

Israel is guilty, says Hosea, of lack of fidelity or faithfulness, of "kindness" (this is the *ḥesed,* the "steadfast love" of 2:16-23 above), and, finally, of there being "no knowledge of God in the land." What is this "knowledge of God"? Obviously, it has nothing to do with an intellectual or theoretical concept of God, with an orthodoxy of any kind. Like all these other terms it refers not to a quality of mind, an intellectual virtue, but to a quality of doing, a way of action. The converse of the "knowledge of God," that is, the refusal to acknowledge what is the way of God, appears in the following v 2: it consists in swearing, lying, killing, stealing, adultery, and murder. In keeping with the common prophetic viewpoint (cf. Amos 1:2), Hosea assumes (v 3) that the current desolation visited on field and stream is the fault of the human inhabitants who are their custodians.

AGAINST THE PRIESTS
4:4-19

 [4] Yet let no one contend, and let none accuse,
   for with you is my contention, O priest.
 [5] You shall stumble by day,
   the prophet also shall stumble with you by night;
   and I will destroy your mother.
 [6] My people are destroyed for lack of knowledge;
   because you have rejected knowledge,
   I reject you from being a priest to me.
   And since you have forgotten the law of your God,
   I also will forget your children.
 [7] The more they increased,
   the more they sinned against me;
   I will change their glory into shame.
 [8] They feed on the sin of my people;
   they are greedy for their iniquity.
 [9] And it shall be like people, like priest;
   I will punish them for their ways,
   and requite them for their deeds.
 [10] They shall eat, but not be satisfied;
   they shall play the harlot, but not multiply;
   because they have forsaken the Lord
   to cherish harlotry.
 [11] Wine and new wine
   take away the understanding.
 [12] My people inquire of a thing of wood,
   and their staff gives them oracles.
   For a spirit of harlotry has led them astray,
   and they have left their God to play the harlot.
 [13] They sacrifice on the tops of the mountains,
   and make offerings upon the hills,
   under oak, poplar, and terebinth,
   because their shade is good.

Therefore your daughters play the harlot,
and your brides commit adultery.
14 I will not punish your daughters when they play the
harlot,
nor your brides when they commit adultery;
for the men themselves go aside with harlots,
and sacrifice with cult prostitutes,
and a people without understanding shall come to
ruin.
15 Though you play the harlot, O Israel,
let not Judah become guilty.
Enter not into Gilgal,
nor go up to Beth-aven,
and swear not, "As the Lord lives."
16 Like a stubborn heifer,
Israel is stubborn;
can the Lord now feed them
like a lamb in a broad pasture?
17 Ephraim is joined to idols, let him alone.
18 A band of drunkards, they give themselves to
harlotry;
they love shame more than their glory.
19 A wind has wrapped them in its wings,
and they shall be ashamed because of their altars.

Whatever may have been the disparate origins of these
prophetic verses, they fit together here in a collective
assault on the Israelite priesthood for its manifold sins.
Not all the verses, to be sure, concern priests specifically,
but v 9 indicates the principle which the prophet or compiler has followed throughout: the responsibility for the
sins of the people must be laid squarely at the door of the
priesthood. The people are destroyed for lack of knowledge (v 1), the knowledge which it was the obligation of
the priests to transmit to their charges. In v 5 "the prophet"

is mentioned along with "the priest" in the same breath: "the prophet" is none other than the type of person that Amaziah considered Amos to be (cf. Amos 7:10), namely the professional figure that was part of the paraphernalia of Israelite religious instruction.

Unlike Amos, Hosea makes a direct connection between the official religion and popular ethical practice. Whereas Amos found the latter to be in glaring hypocritical contrast with the lofty pretensions of the former, Hosea, perhaps more perceptively, sees the former to be actively contributory to all that is wrong in Israel.

The drunkenness (v 11), superstitious divination (v 12), sacrifice in the old pagan sites of recourse (v 13), and practice of the ancient fertility rites of Canaan (vv 13b-14) all contribute to the demoralization of a people. Here is a people that has assimilated itself to the land of its sojourning at the expense of discarding the peculiar spirit that had called it into its distinct existence and identity, and here is a priesthood which has betrayed its responsibility to maintain Israelite identity and has instead encouraged Israel and Canaan to become one.

ISRAEL'S LEADERS
5:1-7

> 5 Hear this, O priests!
>   Give heed, O house of Israel!
>   Hearken, O house of the king!
>   For the judgment pertains to you;
>   for you have been a snare at Mizpah,
>   and a net spread upon Tabor.
> ² And they have made deep the pit of Shittim;
>   but I will chastise all of them.
> ³ I know Ephraim,

and Israel is not hid from me;
for now, O Ephraim, you have played the harlot,
Israel is defiled.
⁴ Their deeds do not permit them
to return to their God.
For the spirit of harlotry is within them,
and they know not the Lord.
⁵ The pride of Israel testifies to his face;
Ephraim shall stumble in his guilt;
Judah also shall stumble with them.
⁶ With their flocks and herds they shall go
to seek the Lord,
but they will not find him;
he has withdrawn from them.
⁷ They have dealt faithlessly with the Lord;
for they have borne alien children.
Now the new moon shall devour them with their
fields.

The indictment continues, now extended not only to the priesthood but also to the "house of the king," that is, to all the officialdom of the kingdom. This seems to be a section in which Israel's politicians are being brought to the dock—we must bear in mind that in the eighth-century Israel of Hosea the "establishment" would have included priests, (official) prophets, and sages (royal counselors, politicians) indifferently. Mizpah, Tabor, and Shittim (vv 1-2) are all well-known places, but why are they mentioned here? Though we have no way of knowing, in view of the lack of information we possess about the history of the times, we may suspect that they represent in this instance recent political disasters that had demoralized the country, in the manner of "Watergate," or "Viet Nam," or "Dien Bien Phu."

DISASTROUS WAR
5:8-15

⁸ Blow the horn in Gibeah,
    the trumpet in Ramah.
    Sound the alarm at Beth-aven;
    tremble, O Benjamin!
⁹ Ephraim shall become a desolation
    in the day of punishment;
    among the tribes of Israel
    I declare what is sure.
¹⁰ The princes of Judah have become
    like those who remove the landmark;
    upon them I will pour out
    my wrath like water.
¹¹ Ephraim is oppressed, crushed in judgment,
    because he was determined to go after vanity.
¹² Therefore I am like a moth to Ephraim,
    and like dry rot to the house of Judah.
¹³ When Ephraim saw his sickness,
    and Judah his wound,
    then Ephraim went to Assyria,
    and sent to the great king.
    But he is not able to cure you
    or heal your wound.
¹⁴ For I will be like a lion to Ephraim,
    and like a young lion to the house of Judah.
    I, even I, will rend and go away,
    I will carry off, and none shall rescue.
¹⁵ I will return again to my place,
    until they acknowledge their guilt
    and seek my face,
    and in their distress they seek me, . . .

The "political" interpretation of 5:1-7 seems to be corroborated by these verses that have been put in sequence. What appears to be in question is the so-called Syro-Ephraimite war, an episode which took place around 733 B.C. The occasion was the attempt of a coalition of small Near Eastern powers to resist Assyrian hegemony under Tiglat-Pileser III. The northern kingdom of Israel and various Aramean states, among others, formed the coalition, into which they tried to coerce the participation of Judah (cf. 2 Kgs 16:5, Isa 7:1). Judah, however, refused to join the coalition and chose what it thought was the better part of prudence, to seek a close alliance with Assyria (2 Kgs 16:7-8). Thus came about the war between Israel and Judah. It is rather naïve to suggest, as some commentators have, that these verses cannot refer to a Syro-Ephraimite war since in v 10 Judah is named as the aggressor. This is like asking for a world history in which every international controversy will have been resolved to the satisfaction of the proverbial disinterested observer. Isaiah, a Judahite, reported the war from his standpoint (cf. Isa 7:1-9), and so it was reported in the largely Judahite record that is the Hebrew OT. Hosea sees the situation differently. He sees the war, in any case, not as a cause for joy, a thing to be remembered, but rather as a symbol of doom. All that has been presaged in the past can only be fulfilled in the future.

REPENTANCE
6:1-6

Saying,

6 "Come, let us return to the Lord;
for he has torn, that he may heal us;
he has stricken, and he will bind us up.
[2] After two days he will revive us;
on the third day he will raise us up,

that we may live before him.

³ Let us know, let us press on to know the Lord;
   his going forth is sure as the dawn;
   he will come to us as the showers,
      as the spring rains that water the earth."
⁴ What shall I do with you, O Ephraim?
   What shall I do with you, O Judah?
   Your love is like a morning cloud,
      like the dew that goes early away.
⁵ Therefore I have hewn them by the prophets,
   I have slain them by the words of my mouth,
      and my judgment goes forth as the light.
⁶ For I desire steadfast love and not sacrifice,
      the knowledge of God, rather than burnt offerings.

One thing that differentiates Hosea from Amos, as we have seen, is his cheerful assumption that there is yet a hope for Israel, that all is not yet lost. This is an interesting phenomenon, for we have no way of deciding which in this situation was the "true" prophet. All that we can say is that Hosea in these verses has produced some of the most poignant lines that are to be attributed to Israelite prophecy, expressive of a subtlety of relationship of God and people which Amos may have missed.

First, the people speak. The Lord has afflicted us, they say, but only for our good. Surely he will—in a day or two or three—surely he will restore us to his favor. (The "third day" of v 2, here simply a vague figure for a future hoped-for redemption, is a not infrequent designation in Scripture of the time of deliverance, cf. Gen 42:18, 2 Kgs 20:5, Jonah 1:17, 2:10, etc., which finds a reflection in the third-day tradition of the Resurrection of Christ in the NT.) What is needed only is that we *know* the Lord. There is no reason to think that the "knowledge" of God has any other than the pregnant sense it has elsewhere in Hosea (cf.

2:10.22, 4:1.6, 5:4). Or in other words, there is no reason to think that what is ascribed to the people in these verses envisions anything other than a genuine repentance, the acceptance of God's moral presence on its own terms.

Thus the poignancy of the following verses, which have appropriately been termed an expression of "divine passion." The intensity of this passion increases in the following verses and chapters. Hosea senses that it *pains* God to deal harshly with a recalcitrant people. He wants to prosper this people, yet he knows how ephemeral is its devotion to "steadfast love" *(ḥesed)* and "the knowledge of God," hard conditions of life to fulfill in contrast with the easy options of the mouth-honor of official civil religion. The Lord welcomes, but he is not so naïve as to be made giddy by Israel's protestations of repentance.

NATIONAL DISASTER
6:7-7:2

⁷ But at Adam they transgressed the covenant;
   there they dealt faithlessly with me.
⁸ Gilead is a city of evildoers,
   tracked with blood.
⁹ As robbers lie in wait for a man,
   so the priests are banded together;
   they murder on the way to Shechem,
   yea, they commit villainy.
¹⁰ In the house of Israel I have seen a horrible thing;
   Ephraim's harlotry is there, Israel is defiled.
¹¹ For you also, O Judah, a harvest is appointed.
   When I would restore the fortunes of
   my people,
7 ¹ when I would heal Israel,
   the corruption of Ephraim is revealed,

> and the wicked deeds of Samaria;
> for they deal falsely,
> the thief breaks in,
> and the bandits raid without.
> [2] But they do not consider
> that I remember all their evil works.
> Now their deeds encompass them,
> they are before my face.

Israel is indeed in a parlous state. Various places are mentioned where atrocities have taken place: Adam, Gilead, Shechem, Samaria. It is neither within our power nor to any purpose to try to determine what were the specific enormities with which the prophet was engaged. Suffice it to say that Hosea has probably registered in these verses a commentary on the social anarchy that attended the Northern Kingdom of Israel as it approached its dissolution at the hands of the Assyrian empire around 722 B.C. That Israel, a tiny state caught between the great pincers of Egypt and Mesopotamia, should have suffered political extinction from without was entirely understandable; that it should have destroyed itself from within, was the incomprehensible.

A PLAGUE ON BOTH YOUR HOUSES
7:3-7

> [3] By their wickedness they make the king glad,
> and the princes by their treachery.
> [4] They are all adulterers;
> they are like a heated oven,
> whose baker ceases to stir the fire,
> from the kneading of the dough
> until it is leavened.

⁵ On the day of our king the princes
   became sick with the heat of wine;
   he stretched out his hand with mockers.
⁶ For like an oven their hearts burn
   with intrigue;
   all night their anger smolders;
   in the morning it blazes like a flaming fire.
⁷ All of them are hot as an oven,
   and they devour their rulers.
   All their kings have fallen;
   and none of them calls upon me.

As should have become evident by now, the charismatic people we call the prophets could be highly political. They were not necessarily effective politically, nor were they always necessarily "right" in their political judgments (for prophecy is always a little larger than life and sometimes exaggerates life), but there was never any doubt as to where they stood.

The verses under consideration are obscure, both because the Book of Hosea itself has been damaged in transmission and because these verses comment on events about which we have very little independent information. What seems to be involved is one or more *coups d'état,* palace revolutions, or attempted regicides perpetrated in the declining days of the northern kingdom by persons unidentified, or identified in a code language to which we have lost the key, and under circumstances which are totally unretrievable by us. Hosea was no friend of the monarchy (cf. 8:4), but he was even less hospitable to anarchy, and it was anarchy that characterized Israel in its latter days preparatory to the final obsequies that would soon be pronounced by the Assyrians. Amos had, already in the heyday of Jeroboam II's illusory prosperity, spoken of Israel as a "ruin" (cf. Amos 6:6). Hosea can now document the reality of the ruin in political terms. There is nothing to choose between king and anti-king, between one or the other faction that tried to prevail in these decaying times. Yahweh and those who would align themselves with Yahweh had nothing to count on from any of them.

INTERNATIONAL POLITICS
7:8-16

[8] Ephraim mixes himself with the peoples;
   Ephraim is a cake not turned.
[9] Aliens devour his strength,
   and he knows it not;
   gray hairs are sprinkled upon him,
   and he knows it not.
[10] The pride of Israel witnesses against him;
   yet they do not return to the Lord their God;
   nor seek him, for all this.
[11] Ephraim is like a dove,
   silly and without sense, calling to Egypt,
   going to Assyria.
[12] As they go, I will spread over them my net;
   I will bring them down like birds of the air;
   I will chastise them for their wicked deeds.
[13] Woe to them, for they have strayed from me!
   Destruction to them, for they have rebelled against me!
   I would redeem them,
   but they speak lies against me.
[14] They do not cry to me from the heart,
   but they wail upon their beds;
   for grain and wine they gash themselves,
   they rebel against me.

¹⁵ Although I trained and strengthened their arms,
yet they devise evil against me.
¹⁶ They turn to Baal,
they are like a treacherous bow,
their princes shall fall by the sword
because of the insolence of their tongue.
This shall be their derision in the land of Egypt.

The political motif continues. How the hardheaded statesmen of Israel must have alternatively gnashed their teeth or shook their tolerant heads over the incredible naïveté of a prophet who proclaimed all of their stratagems inutile! How frustrated they must have been that a political innocent like Hosea should have been permitted, because of the popular awe in which prophecy was held, to contradict with impunity the delicate treaties and alliances which Israel's diplomats had negotiated with such effort and anguish. In a later date—in the time of Jeremiah in Judah—the politicians would find ways of silencing prophecy.

To be sure, Hosea is no man of compromise, no one to acquiesce in wishy-washy views about questions having more than one side. For him Ephraim—the only Israel that is left—is half-baked, callow, stupid in its conceit that by making itself available alternatively to Assyria or Egypt, the two superpowers of the age, or by coyly playing one off against the other in a posture of "nonalignment," it was profitting itself rather than the movers and shakers who toyed with it contemptuously. Ephraim is a silly dove, says Hosea, that brainless, trusting little bird so easily enticed by the snarer. So much for the craftiness of Israelite statesmanship. And in vv 14-16 the prophet probably enraged the politicians the most by suddenly dragging religion into the area of statecraft. Whatever may be the "beds" of v 14, there is no doubt that with the "grain and wine" (cf.

2:8), not to mention the Baal of v 16, Hosea is charging the rulers of Israel with national apostasy, with having adopted the ways of Canaan which once had yielded to the ways of Israel and cannot be a model for the ways of the future. "This shall be their derision in the land of Egypt." Is this a reference to some abortive mission to Egypt in these confused and lawless times?

THE CALF OF SAMARIA
8:1-14

8 Set the trumpet to your lips,
　for a vulture is over the house of the Lord,
　because they have broken my covenant,
　and transgressed my law.
² To me they cry,
　My God, we Israel know thee.
³ Israel has spurned the good;
　the enemy shall pursue him.
⁴ They made kings, but not through me.
　They set up princes, but without my knowledge.
　With their silver and gold they made idols
　for their own destruction.
⁵ I have spurned your calf, O Samaria.
　My anger burns against them.
　How long will it be
　till they are pure ⁶in Israel?
　A workman made it; it is not God.
　The calf of Samaria shall be broken to pieces.
⁷ For they sow the wind,
　and they shall reap the whirlwind.
　The standing grain has no heads,
　it shall yield no meal;
　if it were to yield,

aliens would devour it.

⁸ Israel is swallowed up;
already they are among the nations
as a useless vessel.

⁹ For they have gone up to Assyria,
a wild ass wandering alone;
Ephraim has hired lovers.

¹⁰ Though they hire allies among the nations,
I will soon gather them up.
And they shall cease for a little while
from anointing king and princes.

¹¹ Because Ephraim has multiplied altars
for sinning,
they have become to him altars for sinning.

¹² Were I to write for him my laws by ten thousands,
they would be regarded as a strange thing.

¹³ They love sacrifice;
they sacrifice flesh and eat it;
but the Lord has no delight in them.
Now he will remember their iniquity,
and punish their sins;
they shall return to Egypt.

¹⁴ For Israel has forgotten his Maker,
and built palaces;
and Judah has multiplied fortified cities;
but I will send a fire upon his cities,
and it shall devour his strongholds.

Hosea continues to be sensitive to the connection between the ritual and the moral in the life of the people. Unlike Amos, he invokes the ancient Semitic idea of covenant to describe the terms of the relationship between God and Israel.

"Covenant" in English comes through the French, a "coming together." The word is in current usage, usually to indicate a mutual agreement, a contract. Sometimes that is also the meaning of the Hebrew *berith* that underlies the English "covenant" in the Bible, but not ordinarily. It was in this sometimes sense that the Canaanites and other heathen made covenant with their deities (cf. the Baal-berith of Judg 8:33): they contracted with the national god to render homage and cult in return for protection against their enemies and for the fertility of their soil. This fact explains, perhaps, why a prophet like Amos avoided the term, since the covenant between Yahweh and Israel as the prophets understood it was a quite different matter.

Covenant, in the prophetic and best biblical acceptation, is always an action of divine mercy, in which God and not the people took the initiative. It can be a divine oath, a promise, a pure act of grace given without conditions (as in Gen 12:1-9), or it can be, without ceasing to be an act of grace, an arrangement by which Yahweh has chosen a people to be uniquely his, has showered upon this people manifestations of his saving power, and has imposed on it a code of conduct by which it would be privileged to mirror in its life some approximation of the human ideal. That is the situation here.

After an exordium asserting the theme of a corrupted, rotted Israel, Hosea specifies quite concretely in what ways the covenant of the Lord has been broken and his law transgressed. First, the monarchical establishment (v 4a). Whether he intended to reject the whole succession of Israelite kings or to condemn some of them selectively in view of the breakdown of order that was now taking place, is not clear. In the balance, in any case, the institution had been a disaster which was also apostasy from the covenant. It is by no chance that joined to this count is the contempt expressed for "the calf of Samaria" (vv 4b-6). According to 1 Kgs 12:25-33 it was Jeroboam I of Israel, its first king after the separation of the two kingdoms, who established at Dan and Bethel rival cults of Yahweh under the symbol of a golden calf or bull. Actually, the worship at these ancient shrines (cf. Gen 28:10-22, Judg 18:27-31) had more venerable roots than the Deuteronomic author of 1 Kings would readily acknowledge. But there was no doubt that the Israelite monarchy had identified itself with this "schismatic" cult, and the observances there had encouraged syncretism with the religion of Canaan and blurred the image of the one God of Israel.

Second, there is the matter of foreign alliances (vv 7-10). It should be noted, of course, that "alliance," "treaty," "covenant," and the like, would all have been handled by the one Hebrew word *berith*. Condemnation of foreign ties is frequent in the prophets. Partly it is motivated by the detestation of the anti-Israelite ideas that such alliances introduced into the Israelite sphere (cf. 1 Kgs. 11:1-8, 2 Kgs 16:10-16). More radically, however, it was motivated by the recognition that apostasy had been committed by the intrusion into Israel of an alien covenant, that thereby the Lord of Israel's true covenant had been repudiated. There is no doubt that Israel's statesmen and politicians, themselves not necessarily evil men, would have considered such prophetic viewpoints unrealistic and unwarranted, the illusions of amateurs. There is no doubt, also, about the prophets' usual assessment of the alleged astuteness of Israel's politicians.

The final verses seem to be speaking of useless sacrifices that were preferred to the true worship that consists in observance of the moral law—a not infrequent prophetic sarcasm that here may be again connected with the influence of foreign alliances. The final v 14 looks like a later addition to the text, a fairly stereotyped one.

EXILE
9:1-6

9 Rejoice not, O Israel!
  Exult not like the peoples;

for you have played the harlot, forsaking your God.
You have loved a harlot's hire
upon all threshing floors.
² Threshing floor and winevat shall not feed them,
  and the new wine shall fail them.
³ They shall not remain in the land of the Lord;
but Ephraim shall return to Egypt,
and they shall eat unclean food in Assyria.
⁴ They shall not pour libations of wine
to the Lord;
and they shall not please him with
their sacrifices.
Their bread shall be like mourners' bread;
all who eat of it shall be defiled;
for their bread shall be for their hunger only;
it shall not come to the house of the Lord.
⁵ What will you do on the day of
appointed festival,
and on the day of the feast of the Lord?
⁶ For behold, they are going to Assyria;
Egypt shall gather them,
Memphis shall bury them.
Nettles shall possess their precious things of silver;
thorns shall be in their tents.

Not much is added by these verses to what we have already seen: they are, of course, parallel to various other passages in which foreign exile has been predicted—whether in Egypt or in Assyria is immaterial. The practical consequences are also the same: the failure of the fruits of the land, the cessation of sacrifices and of the traditional religious observances, the dissolution of the people.

VINDICATION OF PROPHECY
9:7-9

> [7] The days of punishment have come,
> the days of recompense have come;
> Israel shall know it.
> The prophet is a fool,
> the man of the spirit is mad,
> because of your great iniquity
> and great hatred.
> [8] The prophet is the watchman of Ephraim,
> the people of my God,
> yet a fowler's snare is on all his ways,
> and hatred in the house of his God.
> [9] They have deeply corrupted themselves
> as in the days of Gibeah:
> he will remember their iniquity,
> he will punish their sins.

"The days of punishment have come," says Hosea triumphantly. Why triumphantly? Because the "wise" of Israel had made it current coin that "the prophet is a fool, the man of the spirit is mad." By now it must have been made evident to anyone who would see that indeed the prophet was not a fool and that what he had prophesied would truly come to pass, however unpleasant it would be both to himself and to those whom he had addressed.

The prophet is a watchman (v 8), says Hosea, anticipating passages like Ezek 3:16-21 and 33:1-9, one of whose tasks is to watch for impending doom and to warn the people of it by the blowing of the trumpet (so Hos 8:1). Hosea has performed his duty and he has gone unheeded. Instead, enormities have been committed, as in the days of Gibeah (Judg 19:30?; cf. Hos 10:9). If this reference has been correctly transmitted, by it the prophet doubtless intends to record a succession of atrocities which has dogged Israel's history.

THE HISTORY OF EPHRAIM
9:10-17

¹⁰ Like grapes in the wilderness, I found Israel.
Like the first fruit on the fig tree,
in its first season,
I saw your fathers.
But they came to Baal-peor,
and consecrated themselves to Baal,
and became detestable like the thing they loved.
¹¹ Ephraim's glory shall fly away like a bird—
no birth, no pregnancy, no conception!
¹² Even if they bring up children,
I will bereave them till none is left.
Woe to them when I depart from them!
¹³ Ephraim's sons, as I have seen, are
destined for a prey;
Ephraim must lead forth his sons to slaughter.
¹⁴ Give them, O Lord—
what wilt thou give?
Give them a miscarrying womb and dry breasts.
¹⁵ Every evil of theirs is in Gilgal;
there I began to hate them.
Because of the wickedness of their deeds
I will drive them out of my house.
I will love them no more;
all their princes are rebels.
¹⁶ Ephraim is stricken,
their root is dried up, they shall bear no fruit.
Even though they bring forth,
I will slay their beloved children.
¹⁷ My God will cast them off,

because they have not hearkened to him;
they shall be wanderers among the nations.

There are two prophetic concepts of the relation of
Yahweh to his people Israel, and the two of them are not
mutually exclusive. In the first of them, which is possibly
the more common, Yahweh is represented as simultane-
ously the creator and savior of his people: creation and salvation are one and the same. This is the theme that begins
with the first creation story of the Book of Genesis (Gen
1:1-2:4a) and is most closely identified with the theology of
the Second Isaiah. (Second Isaiah and the P creation story
of Genesis are closely related theologically). The other concept considers Israel to have been a people whom the Lord
found already made but which he then remade (Ezekiel 23,
for example). That is the viewpoint adopted here. Both of
them agree that Israel's history went downhill from the
moment that Yahweh first touched it, not by his fault but
by Israel's.

Two incidents in Israel's history are mentioned. The first
is that of Baal-peor (v 10), an event that is sufficiently
clarified by the traditional account of Num 25:1-5 (there
are other suggestive allusions in the biblical nomenclature
of Deut 3:29, Josh 13:20, etc.). About Gilgal (v 15) we can
only guess: it was a place of syncretistic worship (Hos
4:15) which had also been condemned by Amos (Amos 4:5,
5:5). In both cases Israel's response to Yahweh's grace has
been, to say the least, unsatisfactory. Yahweh's counter-
response, in turn, was predictable and has already been
verified several times over in the prophecy of Hosea.

ISRAEL'S DISOBEDIENCE
10:1-8

10   Israel is a luxuriant vine
that yields its fruit.

The more his fruit increased the more altars he built;
as his country improved he improved his pillars.
² Their heart is false; now they must bear their guilt.
The Lord will break down their altars,
and destroy their pillars.
³ For now they will say:
"We have no king,
for we fear not the Lord,
and a king, what could he do for us?"
⁴ They utter mere words;
with empty oaths they make covenants;
so judgment springs up like poisonous weeds
in the furrows of the field.
⁵ The inhabitants of Samaria tremble
for the calf of Beth-aven.
Its people shall mourn for it,
and its idolatrous priests shall wail over it,
over its glory which has departed from it.
⁶ Yea, the thing itself shall be carried to Assyria,
as tribute to the great king.
Ephraim shall be put to shame,
and Israel shall be ashamed of his idol.
⁷ Samaria's king shall perish,
like a chip on the face of the waters.
⁸ The high places of Aven, the sin of Israel,
shall be destroyed.
Thorn and thistle shall grow up on their altars;
and they shall say to the mountains, Cover us,
and to the hills, Fall upon us.

Nothing new is added in these verses to the indictment
which Hosea has registered against Israel—syncretistic and
depraved rites, perjury, the calf of Bethel, the seduction of
foreign alliances as the false guarantee of security. It
should be observed, perhaps, that the Beth-aven of v 5

(literally, "house of emptiness") is a deliberate deformation of Bethel (literally, "house of God"). The holiest shrine of northern Israel is so ridiculed by its greatest prophet.

AGAIN THE HISTORY OF EPHRAIM
10:9-15

9 From the days of Gibeah, you have sinned,
O Israel;
there they have continued.
Shall not war overtake them in Gibeah?
10 I will come against the wayward people
to chastise them;
and nations shall be gathered against them
when they are chastised for their double iniquity.
11 Ephraim was a trained heifer
that loved to thresh,
and I spared her fair neck;
but I will put Ephraim to the yoke,
Judah must plow,
Jacob must harrow for himself.
12 Sow for yourselves righteousness,
reap the fruit of steadfast love;
break up your fallow ground,
for it is the time to seek the Lord,
that he may come and rain salvation upon you.
13 You have plowed iniquity,
you have reaped injustice,
you have eaten the fruit of lies.
Because you have trusted in your chariots
and in the multitude of your warriors,
14 therefore the tumult of war shall arise
among your people,
and all your fortresses shall be destroyed,

> as Shalman destroyed Beth-arbel on the day of battle;
> mothers were dashed in pieces with their children.
> [15] Thus it shall be done to you, O house of Israel,
> because of your great wickedness.
> In the storm the king of Israel
> shall be utterly cut off.

Again certain stages in Israel's deplorable history are ticked off, and about them we know very little. Gibeah in v 9 (cf. Hos 5:8, 9:9) we may suppose once more to refer to the episode reported in Judges 19. If so, it is worth remarking that whereas the author of the supplement to the Book of Judges told the story as a sad one from what he regarded as an era of social lawlessness and tribal permissiveness that had preceded the monarchy, Hosea views it strictly as a mindlessly evil deed done in contravention of the divine moral law. The vagaries of biblical viewpoints we have observed before.

And what of Shalman who destroyed Beth-arbel when "mothers were dashed in pieces with their children" (v 14)? Neither the place nor the person nor the event are known to us. All that is known—and known only from this passage—is that taken together they had become proverbial for some unforgettable happening of unspeakable cruelty. That something like it shall be visited on Israel for its wickedness (v 15), we must conclude was in the prophetic view of just recompense, a true return for equally vicious crimes committed by this people.

THE DIVINE PASSION
11:1-11

> **11**   When Israel was a child, I loved him,
> and out of Egypt I called my son.
> [2] The more I called them,

the more they went from me;
they kept sacrificing to the Baals,
and burning incense to idols.
3 Yet it was I who taught Ephraim to walk,
I took them up in my arms;
but they did not know that I healed them.
4 I led them with cords of compassion,
with the bands of love,
and I became to them as one
who eases the yoke on their jaws,
and I bent down to them and fed them.
5 They shall return to the land of Egypt,
and Assyria shall be their king,
because they have refused to return to me.
6 The sword shall rage against their cities,
consume the bars of their gates,
and devour them in their fortresses.
7 My people are bent on turning away from me;
so they are appointed to the yoke,
and none shall remove it.
8 How can I give you up, O Ephraim!
How can I hand you over, O Israel!
How can I make you like Admah!
How can I treat you like Zeboiim!
My heart recoils within me,
my compassion grows warm and tender.
9 I will not execute my fierce anger,
I will not again destroy Ephraim;
for I am God and not man,
the Holy One in your midst,
and I will not come to destroy.
10 They shall go after the Lord,
he will roar like a lion;
yea, he will roar,
and his sons shall come trembling from the west;

¹¹ they shall come trembling like birds from Egyp'
and like doves from the land of Assyria;
and I will return them to their
homes, says the Lord.

This is one of the most engaging passages of the prophet's work. First of all, we have the tender vision of Yahweh choosing Israel to himself not merely as a people but as a son, a child. The relationship is not that of a lord to his vassals—the relationship underlying some of the covenant formulas of the Ancient Near East—but that of adoption, of a would-be father who takes up an abandoned babe in his arms and attempts to rear it in the ways that he knows are right. There are few other episodes in the OT which are so anthropomorphic, which leave the God-concept so vulnerable to the charge that God is only the best of the human ideals writ large. Possibly only Hosea among the prophets would have been capable of the concept. Possibly today only a parent, and possibly only an adoptive parent, would be able to empathize with it completely.

In any case, skipping over the by now routine assurance of retribution that must follow on Israel's failed performance and undutiful sonship (vv 5-7), we arrive at what in consequence is without doubt the most poignant passage in the prophecy of Hosea and, perhaps, what is also one of the ultimate keys to its meaning.

What are we being told in vv 8-9 of this chapter? We are being told that it *hurts* Yahweh to reject and punish Israel. Again we recognize the anthropomorphism, but would an Amos have been capable of it? Here is a God of justice, certainly, of which there can be no doubt; sentimentality does not enter into the question. But he is also a God of compassion, of a compassion that exceeds the human grasp of what is compassion. A compassion, finally, which transcends all notions of human justice and equity and could be learned by a man only through such an experience as has been recorded in Hosea 1-3.

Condemnation will surely come (vv 10-11), but when it comes it will not be the triumphant vindication of justice predicted by an Amos but rather the sad sundering of family ties dolefully awaited by Hosea.

JACOB-ISRAEL-CANAAN
11:12-12:14

[12] Ephraim has encompassed me with lies,
    and the house of Israel with deceit;
    but Judah is still known by God,
    and is faithful to the Holy One.
12 Ephraim herds the wind,
    and pursues the east wind all day long;
    they multiply falsehood and violence;
    they make a bargain with Assyria,
    and oil is carried to Egypt.
[2] The Lord has an indictment against Judah,
    and will punish Jacob according to his ways,
    and requite him according to his deeds.
[3] In the womb he took his brother by the heel,
    and in his manhood he strove with God.
[4] He strove with the angel and prevailed,
    he wept and sought his favor.
    He met God at Bethel,
    and there God spoke with him—
[5] the Lord the God of hosts,
    the Lord is his name:
[6] "So you, by the help of your God, return,
    hold fast to love and justice,
    and wait continually for your God."
[7] A trader, in whose hands are false balances,

he loves to oppress.

8 Ephraim has said, "Ah, but I am rich,
I have gained wealth for myself";
but all his riches can never offset
the guilt he has incurred.

9 I am the Lord your God
from the land of Egypt;
I will again make you dwell in tents,
as in the days of the appointed feast.

10 I spoke to the prophets;
it was I who multiplied visions,
and through the prophets gave parables.

11 If there is iniquity in Gilead
they shall surely come to nought;
if in Gilgal they sacrifice bulls,
their altars also shall be like stone heaps
on the furrows of the field.

12 (Jacob fled to the land of Aram,
there Israel did service for a wife,
and for a wife he herded sheep.)

13 By a prophet the Lord brought Israel
up from Egypt,
and by a prophet he was preserved.

14 Ephraim has given bitter provocation;
so his Lord will leave his blood-guilt upon him,
and will turn back upon him his reproaches.

In the Hebrew text these are the fifteen verses of chapter 12.

What we have that unites these verses is a fairly elaborate manipulation of Israelite tradition in which eponymous names—names, that is, which serve equally well for supposed ancestors and for the ethnic bodies which are alleged to be their descent—are used indiscriminately and with free crossover from one identity to the other. It is a bit like our using the one name for Washington, George, and Washington, DC (and recognizing a connection between the two); though of course we know that "the father of his country" was not literally the ancestor of his countrymen.

We can skip over 11:12a, which says nothing that has not been voiced previously. (It should be obvious by now that 11:12b is the product of a hopeful postexilic Judahite redaction of Hosea's prophecies.) We can also skip over 12:1, which does little more than repeat in other language what was said by 11:12a. We shall consider only the new ideas which are asserted in v 2 and the following.

Even here we have to make a slight reservation. The "Judah" of v 2 undoubtedly substitutes for an original "Israel": another Judahite adaptation after Hosea's prophetic words had been imported into the south. The names "Israel" and "Jacob," eponymous and personal, we may recall are frequently interchangeable in the Genesis patriarchal story. What is far more important is that in these verses we are confronted, from the viewpoint of a northern prophet, with the portrait of an ancient ancestral figure passed into legend which stands in considerable contrast with the view of him reflected in the Book of Genesis (which is, ultimately, a southern or Judahite refraction of Israel's formative traditions). Add to this the consideration that the Jacob/Israel tradition was doubtless originally the property of northern rather than southern elements of the tribes who formed the confederation and later nation of Israel. Variations in northern and southern versions of the resultant common tradition should not surprise us. Probably we have already seen an example of this, a minor one, in 11:8 above. There Admah and Zeboiim are featured as proverbial cities of disaster. They are hardly mentioned elsewhere in Scripture except in Genesis 14 and 19 and a parallel in Deut 29:22. There they figure as only two of the five "cities of the plain" destroyed by God's wrath. In the Judahite version of the story, however—not only in Genesis but also in Isa 1:9, Jer 49:18, Zeph 2:9, etc.—it is not Admah and Zeboiim but rather two other of the cities, Sodom and Gomorrah, which figure in the proverb.

Hosea announces that Yahweh has an "indictment" against Jacob and will punish him for "ways" which in the Genesis narrative are detailed at least dispassionately and probably even with implied commendation. The "ways" of Jacob: he took his brother by the heel in his mother's womb (cf. Gen 25:26); he strove with God (cf. Gen 32:23-33); he met God at Bethel (cf. Gen 28:13); he went to Aram where he served for two wives (cf. Gen 29:15-30), etc. There is no doubt that the traditions are common, but for Hosea, unlike Genesis, the story has become paradigmatic of Israel's present state of restlessness, fickleness, rebelliousness, and irresponsibility. Like father, like son.

So in v 7—probably another eponym. The "trader" of *RSV* is also the Hebrew word "Canaan." Jacob/Israel/Ephraim has also become Canaan, and has in turn adopted the mores of that mercantile society in preference to the covenant law of Israel (cf. Amos 8:4-6). As Amos did (Amos 2:11), Hosea reminds Israel of the charismatic presence of prophecy which should have, but had not, kept it distinct as a peculiar people (v 10). Unlike Amos (in v 11), he also continues to recognize the intimate connection between popular religious observance and popular moral practice. And again unlike Amos (in v 9), his message of retribution to Israel describes it as medicinal rather than simply a sentence of doom. That Israel shall again "dwell in tents, as in the days of the appointed feast," means that there is for Israel the hope of a new exodus, a renewed time of innocence and probation, from which it can emerge as the people that it was once meant to be.

The prophet by whom Yahweh brought Israel up from Egypt (v 13) is certainly Moses. Who is the prophet by whom Israel was—in hope if not in fact—"preserved"? Probably, the same Moses. The tradition which attached Israel's convenantal law to Moses was far more ancient than the final redaction of the Pentateuch that made it an article of dogma.

MEN KISS CALVES!
13:1-3

13 When Ephraim spoke, men trembled;
   he was exalted in Israel;
   but he incurred guilt through Baal and died.
² And now they sin more and more,
   and make for themselves molten images,
   idols skilfully made of their silver,
   all of them the work of craftsmen.
   Sacrifice to these, they say.
   Men kiss calves!
³ Therefore they shall be like the morning mist
   or like the dew that goes early away,
   like the chaff that swirls from the
   threshing floor
   or like smoke from a window.

Here nothing much of substance is added to what Hosea has otherwise uttered with regard to Ephraim's retrograde religion, compounded of the contamination of its tradition with the practices of Canaan and the worship of Baal. If there is any additional contribution, it is only that of sarcasm: Men kiss calves!

THE SHEPHERD AND THE LION
13:4-11

⁴ I am the Lord your God
   from the land of Egypt;
   you know no God but me,
   and besides me there is no savior.
⁵ It was I who knew you in the wilderness,
   in the land of drought;
⁶ but when they had fed to the full,
   they were filled, and their heart was lifted up;
   therefore they forgot me.
⁷ So I will be to them like a lion,
   like a leopard I will lurk beside the way.
⁸ I will fall upon them like a bear
   robbed of her cubs,
   I will tear open their breast,
   and there I will devour them like a lion,
   as a wild beast would rend them.
⁹ I will destroy you, O Israel;
   who can help you?
¹⁰ Where now is your king, to save you;
   where are all your princes, to defend you—
   those of whom you said,
   "Give me a king and princes"?
¹¹ I have given you kings in my anger,
   and I have taken them away in my wrath.

Yahweh, who first met with Israel in the wilderness (Hos
9:10) or in Egypt (Hos 11:1), and thenceforth became its
shepherd of guidance, now declares himself the lion,
leopard, bear, or other wild beast whose habit it is to prey
on the flock which the shepherd guards. The fault for this
reversal of roles is, of course, Israel's.

The final verses are a taunt. Previously (8:4) Hosea has

denigrated Israel's monarchy as a bad idea. Here he concedes, as he must, that it could never have been had not Yahweh willed it (v 11). But he willed it, says the prophet, only as a proleptic sign of the doom that now descends upon the land. And a paradoxical sign it is as well. The common sense and *Realpolitik* in which the people have trusted have now been demonstrated to lead to nothing but disaster. Prophecy—whose alternatives had never been tested—could afford to be complacent as the little kingdom now began to come crashing down upon recusant heads.

ISRAEL IS CONDEMNED
13:12-16

[12] The iniquity of Ephraim is bound up,
    his sin is kept in store.
[13] The pangs of childbirth come for him,
    but he is an unwise son;
    for now he does not present himself
    at the mouth of the womb.
[14] Shall I ransom them from the power of Sheol?
    Shall I redeem them from Death?
    O Death, where are your plagues?
    O Sheol, where is your destruction?
    Compassion is hid from my eyes.
[15] Though he may flourish as the reed plant,
    the east wind, the wind of the Lord, shall come,
    rising from the wilderness;
    and his fountain shall dry up,
    his spring shall be parched;
    it shall strip his treasury
    of every precious thing.
[16] Samaria shall bear her guilt,

because she has rebelled against her God;
they shall fall by the sword,
their little ones shall be dashed in pieces,
and their pregnant women ripped open.

This is one of the most typical passages of the OT, in the sense that what is apodictically asserted in these verses will be apparently immediately contradicted by the verses which follow in the next chapter. This phenomenon is not a pointer to disparate authorship; it is rather a result of something most congenial to the Semitic mind and therefore to the expression of the Hebrew OT. To understand the single mentality that produced both of these passages, one must recognize that quality of the Hebrew OT which G. B. Caird has characterized as "a tendency to think in extremes without qualification."

In other words, in these verses under discussion, there is an absolute and total repudiation of Israel by Yahweh done in meticulous detail, a summary of much that has gone before which also conflicts with much that follows. (Whether v 16, in the Hebrew text 14:1, referring to Samaria is original with Hosea or is the work of a later author sensitive to the division between Jews and Samaritans which occurred before the final edition of the OT, can be disputed.)

RETURN, O ISRAEL
14:1-8

14 Return, O Israel, to the Lord your God,
for you have stumbled because of your iniquity.
² Take with you words
and return to the Lord;
say to him,
"Take away all iniquity;

accept that which is good
and we will render
the fruit of our lips.
³ Assyria shall not save us,
we will not ride upon horses;
and we will say no more, 'Our God,'
to the work of our hands.
In thee the orphan finds mercy."
⁴ I will heal their faithlessness;
I will love them freely,
for my anger has turned from them.
⁵ I will be as the dew to Israel;
he shall blossom as the lily,
he shall strike root as the poplar;
⁶ his shoots shall spread out;
his beauty shall be like the olive,
and his fragrance like Lebanon.
⁷ They shall return and dwell beneath my shadow,
they shall flourish as a garden;
they shall blossom as the vine,
their fragrance shall be like the wine of Lebanon.
⁸ O Ephraim, what have I to do with idols?
It is I who answer and look after you.
I am like an evergreen cypress,
from me comes your fruit.

These verses are 14:2-9 in the Hebrew text and in the *New American Bible.* They issue a clear invitation to Israel to return to the Lord, in return for which everything will be forgiven. How different were the words of Amos, for whom there was no return! Why, asks Hosea, should there be any problem, when the way of salvation is so obvious and clear? Return to the Lord: do good and not evil (cf. Mic 6:8). Repudiate the foreign entanglements that have

sapped away at authentic religious roots (v 3). Repudiate
the cheap nationalistic religion that stops at mouth honor
and painless ritual, and instead make justice and right
prevail (v 3, cf. Isa 1:23, 10:2). For every faithlessness
there is a remedy, and the remedy is "return." To return is
to turn around, and in Hebrew "return" *(shûb)* can also
mean "repent." The Septuagint sometimes translated the
Hebrew verb with the Greek *metanoiein,* which etymologi-
cally means "to change the mind." When the NT (as in
Acts 20:21, "repentance to God") speaks, as it so often
does, of *metanoia,* we can hear the Semitic "return" and
"turn around" of its origins.

"What have I to do with idols" in v 8 should be taken
less as a question than as an exclamation. It is, indeed, a
statement of revulsion. All promises of the fertility gods of
Canaan have proved to be empty and vain. It is Yahweh
and not the gods of Canaan who has preserved Israel on
Canaanite soil, and that Israel has not understood this fact
is the best evidence of its need for salvation.

ENVOY
14:9

> [9] Whoever is wise, let him understand
>   these things;
>   whoever is discerning, let him know them;
>   for the ways of the Lord are right,
>   and the upright walk in them,
>   but transgressors stumble in them.

This is the final verse of the Book of Hosea (v 10 in the
Hebrew text). It is, as everyone acknowledges, a
"wisdom" codicil to the finished work as it finally emerged
from the hands of its editors and redactors. The best commentary we can give it is to note how it testifies that from

the beginning prophetic words were recognized to have perennial validity, by no means to be restricted to the original historical setting that had called them into being.

MICAH

THE TITLE
1:1

> **1** The word of the Lord that came to Micah of
> Moresheth in the days of Jotham, Ahaz, and Hezekiah,
> kings of Judah, which he saw concerning Samaria and
> Jerusalem.

AS IS CUSTOMARY in the Judahite redaction of all the prophetic works, the words of the prophet Micah have been
gathered together under the rubric of the chronology of
Judah's kings, in this instance Jotham, Ahaz, and Hezekiah
(i.e., outside dates of approximately 738-687 B.C.). The
chronology is more appropriate here than elsewhere we
have seen it, since the scene of Amos' and Hosea's activity
was Israel, while as far as we know Micah's prophetic
career was lived out exclusively in Judah. We have independent evidence, on the basis of Jer 26:18-19 (which cites
Mic 3:12), that Micah flourished in the time of Hezekiah.
We can also probably set a date of about 725 B.C. as the
latest when he would have begun to make his voice heard,
since it spoke not only against Judah but against northern
Israel as well, which had not yet sunk into the oblivion
predicted for it. As Hosea succeeded in Israel as a latter-

day Amos, therefore, so did Micah succeed in Judah as a
latter-day Hosea.

JUDGMENT ON SAMARIA
1:2-7

> [2] Hear, you peoples, all of you;
>   hearken, O earth, and all that is in it;
>   and let the Lord God be a witness against you,
>   the Lord from his holy temple.
> [3] For behold, the Lord is coming forth
>   out of his place,
>   and will come down and tread upon
>   the high places of the earth.
> [4] And the mountains will melt under him
>   and the valleys will be cleft,
>   like wax before the fire,
>   like waters poured down a steep place.
> [5] All this is for the transgression of Jacob
>   and for the sins of the house of Israel.
>   What is the transgression of Jacob?
>   Is it not Samaria?
>   And what is the sin of the house of Judah?
>   Is it not Jerusalem?
> [6] Therefore I will make Samaria a heap
>   in the open country,
>   a place for planting vineyards;
>   and I will pour down her stones into the valley,
>   and uncover her foundations.
> [7] All her images shall be beaten to pieces,
>   all her hires shall be burned with fire,
>   and all her idols I will lay waste;
>   for from the hire of a harlot she gathered them,
>   and to the hire of a harlot they shall return.

Indeed, the first verses of Micah's prophecy clearly concern the northern capital of Samaria (captured by the Assyrian king Sargon II in 721 B.C.) more than they do the southern capital of Jerusalem; or perhaps it is more accurate to say that the former is featured as an object lesson to the latter.

"You peoples" originally meant simply Israel and Judah, no doubt, just as the "earth" (the Hebrew means only "the land") referred to the traditional land of promise. (In 1 Kgs 22:28 part of this verse has been ascribed to Micaiah ben Imlah whom a later tradition had evidently identified with Micah of Moresheth.) However, there is ample reason to agree with the later biblical viewpoint that saw this as a universalist proclamation. For one thing, we have already seen that it was no novel thought, particularly for a Judahite prophet, to conceive of Yahweh as the master of other peoples than merely those of the Israelite covenant. Secondly, Yahweh is represented here as a Deity transcendent of this earth, descending from his heavenly temple (cf. Pss 11:4, 29:10), his "place" above (cf. Hos 5:l5, Ps 14:2), to appear in the theophanic majesty of judgment with cosmic consequences (v 4). Language of this kind becomes much more common when it is later incorporated into apocalyptic imagery, but it is also quite ancient in Israel.

Both Jacob/Israel and Judah, epitomized by their respective capitals of Samaria and Jerusalem, are equally condemned. It is Samaria, however, whose end was now in easy view, that is put in the forefront. The language is prophetic, not statistically historical. Samaria was, indeed, conquered, and everything that was threatened against it took place in the spirit in which it was prophesied. It was not, however, reduced to a pile of rubble. Instead, now under other management, it remained a capital city for the

Assyrian conquerors and later for their successors the Persians.

LAMENTATION
1:8-16

8 For this I will lament and wail;
I will go stripped and naked;
I will make lamentation like the jackals,
and mourning like the ostriches.

9 For her wound is incurable;
and it has come to Judah,
it has reached to the gate of my people,
to Jerusalem.

10 Tell it not in Gath,
weep not at all;
in Beth-le-aphrah
roll yourselves in the dust.

11 Pass on your way,
inhabitants of Shaphir,
in nakedness and shame;
the inhabitants of Zaanan
do not come forth;
the wailing of Beth-ezel
shall take away from you its standing place.

12 For the inhabitants of Maroth
wait anxiously for good,
because evil has come down from the Lord
to the gate of Jerusalem.

13 Harness the steeds to the chariots,
inhabitants of Lachish;
you were the beginning of sin
to the daughter of Zion,
for in you were found

the transgressions of Israel.
¹⁴ Therefore you shall give parting gifts
to Moresheth-gath; the houses of Achzib shall be a
deceitful thing
to the kings of Israel.
¹⁵ I will again bring a conqueror upon you,
inhabitants of Mareshah;
the glory of Israel shall come to Adullam.
¹⁶ Make yourselves bald and cut off your hair,
for the children of your delight;
make yourselves as bald as the eagle,
for they shall go from you into exile.

This is possibly the most vexing of all the sections of Micah's prophecy. Vexing because, on the one hand, for various reasons it is probably the most poorly preserved of all these sections and also because, on the other hand, it is precisely in this section that we are put in most authentic contact with the prophet. We shall do the best we can at commentary, following the *RSV* which, in turn, has produced a translation of the text which probably represents the best that can presently be made of it.

Fortunately, the basic ideas of the text do not seem to be in doubt, despite the damage it has endured. First there is prophetic lamentation, limited in this instance to the evils that are to be visited upon the prophet's own Judah (vv 8-9.16). Even Amos could intercede for Israel in the face of Yahweh's verdict of disaster (Amos 7:1-6). Hosea could go further, empathizing with both Israel and its Lord at the imminent prospect of repudiation and devastation (Hos 11:8-9, etc.). Later on, Jeremiah would weep for his condemned people while freely acknowledging all that had brought down the condemnation (Jer 8:22-9:3 in *RSV;* 8:22-9:2 in the Hebrew). We are never allowed to lose sight entirely of the prophet as intercessor, mediator, spokesman for the people as one of the people, though his role as messenger of God is more prominent and paramount.

Secondly, in these verses we are doubtless introduced to the little world of the prophet Micah. You are not likely to find in any single Bible atlas the location on a map of all the dozen places that are named within vv 10-15. Half of them, perhaps. Only two or three are of such consequence as to be mentioned elsewhere in the Bible; the rest (including the Moresheth-gath which was presumably Micah's home town) were simply villages clustering around larger centers like Gath, Hebron, and Lachish in the southwest of Judah, midway between the Dead Sea and the Mediterranean coast, accounting for a pitifully few square miles of this earth. Micah has brought into his lamentation the names of these places he knew from boyhood and in his maturity—possibly the only places of which he had firsthand knowledge—as bearers of the guilt (to be specified in the next chapter) which will call down sure retribution upon Judah.

We have said that these verses are poorly preserved. This fact becomes immediately apparent in v 10. "Gath" itself does not form a problem here, even though some authors have thought it necessary to look for another place name hiding behind the Hebrew, like the Giloh of Josh 15:51, for example, which lay somewhere between Hebron and the Philistine plain. Gath, it is true, was proverbially a Philistine rather than a Judahite city—but not always. The city lay on the march of Philistia and Judah, and the political and ethnic balance frequently changed there, through violence or otherwise; the name Moresheth-gath for an obviously Judahite site indicates well enough that Gath had Judahite resonances in the time of Micah.

What seems to be wrong with this v 10a is "tell it not. . . weep not at all." The redactor of Micah's text may have been beguiled by 2 Sam 1:20, where "tell it not in Gath" makes excellent sense, and, misunderstanding the Mican verse that had come to him, he could have adjusted the one to the other. We can only guess what was originally written, but probably it was something like "rejoice not in Gath" (all that would be needed to produce this sense would be the change of a single Hebrew letter). If this emendation of the text should be justified, then (by the substitution of another single Hebrew letter) the parallel could be appropriately translated "weep exceedingly." With these alterations, the verse fits its context completely.

What Micah is saying is that he sees the towns and villages of his acquaintance emblematic of both the guilt of Judah and of the sure retribution that will overtake it. Some of the details escape us. Why, for example, is Lachish called "the beginning of sin" for Jerusalem? The explicative parallel which speaks of "the transgressions of Israel" does not help much, for we cannot know what transgressions Micah had in mind. Our history fails us, in this respect as in others. Also, this passage is saturated with word-plays (random examples: in v 10 after *beth-le-aphrah* comes *aphar,* "dust"; in v 13 the chariots of Lachish plays on the assonance *larechesh lachish,* etc.). Wordplays are not, as some have peevishly thought in the case of Micah, a sign of low rather than sophisticated literary style. But, as anyone who has ever tried to write within the confines of rhyme or some other controlling structural device knows full well, what might otherwise be conveyed more accurately in pedestrian, wordy prose frequently is rendered opaque by the chosen artistic medium.

THE LATIFUNDISTS
2:1-5

2 Woe to those who devise wickedness
and work evil upon their beds!

> When the morning dawns, they perform it,
> because it is in the power of their hand.
> ² They covet fields, and seize them;
> and houses, and take them away;
> they oppress a man and his house,
> a man and his inheritance.
> ³ Therefore thus says the Lord:
> Behold, against this family I am devising evil,
> from which you cannot remove your necks;
> and you shall not walk haughtily,
> for it will be an evil time.
> ⁴ In that day they shall take up a taunt
> song against you,
> and wail with bitter lamentation,
> and say, "We are utterly ruined;
> he changes the portion of my people;
> how he removes it from me!
> Among our captors he divides our fields."
> ⁵ Therefore you will have none to cast
> the line by lot
> in the assembly of the Lord.

Latifundium is a Latin term derived from *latus* (broad, wide) and *fundus* (cognate with our "fund" = estate, property). It means, therefore, simply a broad estate, a Ponderosa, a King Ranch. But in some Latin countries, and not only in Latin countries, *latifundismo* or its equivalent today denotes not merely the possession of vast estates but also connotes the callous and antisocial means by which such estates have been acquired and are maintained. This, whatever the view simplistic or otherwise concerning the laws of economics or the realities of contemporary social life.

Micah does not use the term latifundism, but it is obvious that it is of this that he is speaking, and it is equally obvious that he is thinking of it in a quite modern way. Big, he says, is bad, and whatever has contributed to bigness is equally bad. There is no superstition here, however, and no rejection of latifundism on grounds that would much appeal to contemporary sociologists or politicians. He condemns it in purely Israelite terms. The latifundists—he caricatures them, surely—are pictured as spending not only their waking hours at exploiting their fellows but also of dreaming devices against them in their sleep (v 1). It would seem that Micah, a man from a little backwater village in Judah, had a very personal animus against these great landowners which seriously influenced his prophecy. Isaiah (cf. 5:8-10) would also echo some of his words, but one has the impression that while Isaiah, the liberal aristocrat, was responding on principle, Micah was anguishing from bitter experience.

The evil of the latifundists, says Micah, is that by their manipulation of the economy they defraud a man of his "inheritance." This word has no truly "secular" meaning. It was the word used by Naboth the Jezreelite according to 1 Kgs 21:3, when in its name that humble Israelite tender of his ancestral vines felt free to refuse the handsome offer made by Ahab, king of Israel, that he should exchange his acres for others in order to accommodate the royal convenience. "Yahweh forbid that I should give you the inheritance of my fathers," said Naboth. It was answer enough, then, to check Ahab's whim. Against Israelite law and custom Ahab had no recourse to *force majeure,* until his Phoenician wife Jezebel instructed him in the ways by which the kings of the Gentiles got their will done.

The "inheritance" of an Israelite was for him not simply what he had inherited from his fathers but from God himself, his share in the land that had been apportioned to Israel at Yahweh's direction (Joshua 12-21 is a late theological simplification of the historical process). This religious interpretation of land possession, national or individual, could be dangerous, of course, and easily abused, since hegemony might be claimed in the name of God when it had actually been acquired only by superior force and conquest. But on the individual basis it was, in general, a fruitful doctrine, protecting in religious terms the nuclear element of society, the family holding which in an agricultural and pastoral way of life was the guarantee of financial independence and therefore of equal rights and dignity in society. The worst fate dreaded by an Israelite was a proletarian polity, in which a dependent class would be declared and thus society become stratified on economic rather than natural or religious grounds.

Appropriately, since the rulers and shakers have disturbed the ancient balance by their latifundist greed, there will come the conqueror who observes neither the old rules nor their own. All that they thought to have gained will be lost, and there will be no redistribution of the land as had been in days of old (vv 4-5).

PROPHESY NOT!
2:6-11

⁶ "Do not preach"—thus they preach—
"one should not preach of such things;
disgrace will not overtake us."
⁷ Should this be said, O house of Jacob?
Is the Spirit of the Lord impatient?
Are these his doings?
Do not my words do good
to him who walks uprightly?
⁸ But you rise against my people as an enemy;
you strip the robe from the peaceful,
from those who pass by trustingly

with no thought of war.

⁹ The women of my people you drive out
  from their pleasant houses;
  from their young children you take away
  my glory for ever.

¹⁰ Arise and go,
   for this is no place to rest;
   because of uncleanness that destroys
   with a grievous destruction.

¹¹ If a man should go about and utter
   wind and lies,
   saying, "I will preach to you of wine
   and strong drink,"
   he would be the preacher for this people!

Prophets do not, notoriously, attract a large and enthusiastic following in their own lifetimes. They have their disciples, it is true, and for lack of these we would probably have none of the prophetic literature preserved for us in the Bible. They also have many fairweather supporters, those who are in sympathy with their efforts and who lend them "moral" support as long as it costs them nothing socially or politically (the Nicodemus of John 3 is a NT paradigm of this sort of character): perhaps these people, too, once the prophet was safely dead, have made their contribution to the enshrinement of his memory. We should, therefore, be grateful to them for the good they have done and even pardon them for their faintheartedness, recognizing in it a quality which we also share.

There are also, finally, those who make up the most vocal element, which will not hear prophecy. Whether they form a majority or a minority makes no difference and cannot be determined; all that can be determined is that they are the most vocal. These are the ones we hear in vv 6-11.

To hear them most clearly, we have to use a little better punctuation than has been employed by *RSV*. In v 6 they say—no contest—that "one should not preach of such things; disgrace will not overtake us." It is a standard retort from a smug and complacent society that has nothing to fear from its tutelary Deity since it has paid its dues and has every reason to expect that there will be a comforting reciprocity on his part. In v 7, however, the quotation undoubtedly continues (these are the additional words of the skeptics): "Can the house of Jacob be accursed?/ Is Yahweh's spirit, then, cut short?/ Could such things be done by him?" These hearers of Micah's words are refusing to believe them, for they cannot accept that Yahweh's protecting power will be withdrawn from them and that they have really been cast off by their God. It is unheard of that Israel can be bereft of Yahweh.

But the unheard of must now be heard. "Do not my words do good," says the Lord, *"only* to him who walks uprightly?" (v 7b). This is the pronouncement of Yahweh against those who profess to be his people. And what is this people in reality? In vv 8-10 they are clearly defined: robbers, exploiters, despoilers, oppressors of the poor and helpless, extortioners of widows and orphans, grand and petty larceners on every scale.

The subject becomes distasteful. The only kind of prophet that this people would be willing to hear, Micah concludes, would be one that proclaimed only windy, consoling platitudes and encouraged the philosophy of *carpe diem.* Hope is not to be retrieved so easily.

RESTORATION
2:12-13

> [12] I will surely gather all of you, O Jacob,
>   I will gather the remnant of Israel;

I will set them together
like sheep in a fold,
like a flock in its pasture,
a noisy multitude of men.
¹³ He who opens the breach will go up before them;
they will break through and pass the gate,
going out by it.
Their king will pass on before them,
the Lord at their head.

Such being Micah's declared disposition, it is hard to ascribe to him these verses that follow in the book. They look very much like the words of some exilic or early postexilic prophet uttered in the spirit of the "book of consolation" of the Second Isaiah (Isaiah 40-55) or the "new Israel" of Ezekiel 40-48. They are a promise of liberation from exile and of restoration. It was common practice of the redactors of the prophetic books to insert passages of this kind which temper preceding words of doom, since the action of the Lord had been ultimately one of salvation once the trials and punishments he had brought upon his people had achieved their purpose.

AGAINST THE RULERS
3:1-4

3 And I said:
Hear, you heads of Jacob
and rulers of the house of Israel!
Is it not for you to know justice?—
² you who hate the good and love the evil,
who tear the skin from off my people,
and their flesh from off their bones;
³ who eat the flesh of my people,
and flay their skin from off them,

> and break their bones in pieces,
> and chop them up like meat in a kettle,
> like flesh in a caldron.
> ⁴ Then they will cry to the Lord,
> but he will not answer them;
> he will hide his face from them at that time,
> because they have made their deeds evil.

Here and in v 9 below one might be tempted by the reiterated Jacob/Israel parallel to conclude, as it was legitimate to conclude in other prophetic passages, that the prophet's purview was the northern kingdom of Israel. And certainly, as we observed in the first chapter of this book above, Micah did have concern for this northern kingdom in the days of its decline. However, v 10 below which adds "Zion" and "Jerusalem" to the parallel, and of which there is no reason whatever to question the authenticity, gives us the clue to the proper interpretation of all the verses. We are now in the period after 722-21 B.C. The northern kingdom has now been absorbed by Assyria and as a political entity has disappeared from the scene. What remains of the Yahwistic community is for all practical purposes only Judah, which now reclaims for itself ancient ancestral names like "Israel." This transition of names is elsewhere verifiable in the OT, and it is not without parallels in the histories of other peoples.

Jer 26:18, which cites Mic 3:12, also probably identifies these verses as well as prophecy directed against Judah in the days of king Hezekiah. It was fearless prophecy—as indeed Jeremiah makes it out to be—since it was addressed, quite obviously, to the highest and mightiest in the kingdom. The terms (v 1) "heads" and "rulers" may be deliberately vague: "head" and "ruler" was the title bestowed on Jephthah according to Judg 11:11. What is meant, undoubtedly, is not only those who had some official, royally sanctioned right to govern, but also, in view of what follows, those who were otherwise sanctioned by tradition or religion to hold positions of authority or prestige which would make them responsible for the course of events. It is the "establishment," in other words, that is under indictment. It is these whose duty it was to know justice: *mishpat* is the word, a word which can mean judicial justice (recall Amos 5:1-17) but also has a highly moral meaning, signifying the way by which Yahweh would have his people walk.

Whatever the precise responsibility to be borne by those who fall under Micah's scrutiny, and whatever the precise details of their shortcomings and transgressions, they fit a common mold. They have cannibalized their people—literally, devouring their substance (judicial connivance is doubtless in view here, the abuse of administrative and police power). They have not only betrayed their trust, they have gloried in their betrayal. Hence they are doomed. They, these bureaucrats and hangers-on who have been so careful to hedge their bets and keep on the winning side, assuredly they shall find themselves at last to be nothing but losers. And the God to whom they have professed pious deference while working their little schemes will regard them with contempt and incomprehension.

THE VAIN PROPHETS
3:5-8

> ⁵ Thus says the Lord concerning the prophets
> who lead my people astray,
> who cry "Peace"
> when they have something to eat,
> but declare war against him
> who puts nothing into their mouths.

⁶ Therefore it shall be night to you
   without vision,
   and darkness to you, without divination.
   The sun shall go down upon the prophets,
   and the day shall be black over them;
⁷ the seers shall be disgraced,
   and the diviners put to shame;
   they shall all cover their lips,
   for there is no answer from God.
⁸ But as for me, I am filled with power,
   with the Spirit of the Lord,
   and with justice and might,
   to declare to Jacob his transgression
   and to Israel his sin.

As in 2:6-11 we have here an interlude on prophecy, except this time the interlude is much more closely connected with what immediately precedes and follows. For the "prophets" here undoubtedly form a major part of that "establishment" whose government and counsels Micah has been and will be condemning in the surrounding verses. They were, as we have seen in our introduction, first of all a long accepted institution in Israel (cf. 1 Sam 9:7-9), "men of God" whose life was supposedly led in close communion with the sphere of the divine and whose word was in consequence regarded, sometimes even superstitiously, as divine oracle (so Nathan in 2 Sam 12:1-15, Elijah in 1 Kgs 21:17-24, the unnamed prophetic emissary in 2 Kgs 9:1-13). And, like many men convinced of a personal, charismatic mission, they were sometimes capable of confusing what they thought they had been sent to do with what it was in their interest to do, or say.

It is this personal interest that Micah now imputes to the prophets of Judah which impels them to proclaim "Peace!" The institution of the professional honorarium for a prophetic word was taken for granted (cf. 1 Sam 9:5-10) and is not being called in question here: Micah would no more have condemned this out of hand than would one of his modern counterparts repudiate in principle that a physician or psychiatrist should live by his profession. What, however, is to be said of the physician who, for consideration other than his client's, assures a cancer-ridden patient that he is indeed in good health? What of the psychiatrist who accepts his fee in exchange for a placebo of advice that returns to society a person dangerously disturbed? We need not interpret too materially the "eat" or "nothing in their mouths" of v 5. There is more than one way of feeding or starving a prophet or any other functionary, and Micah is saying simply that the prophets of Judah have been bought. Like the prophets of peace against whom Jeremiah would later raise his voice (Jer 6:14, 8:11, etc.), these men of insight had been persuaded by offers they could not refuse to reassure a wayward people that no disaster could eventually overwhelm them. To the contrary, it is this eventual disaster that Micah predicts in v 8, the word of one prophet against the many prophets. Characteristically of true prophecy, he can only claim, he cannot prove by any sign, that he and not they possesses "the Spirit of the Lord." True prophecy requires for its validation a corresponding openness to prophecy itself. Faith cannot be compelled; it grows up only in receptive ground.

In these verses about contemporary prophets we encounter terms like "vision" (which goes with the "seer," who is one who "sees" something) and "diviners" and "divination." In later Israelite language these terms become pejorative, implying manipulative processes which a more sophisticated piety deemed to be heathen and retrograde. However, it was the contrast with the long tradition of classical prophets like Micah, who are not normally associated with such devices, that accounts for the later pejorative connotations. The seer (in Amos 1:1, the prophet Amos is named a seer) depended for his visions, pretended or genuine, on second sight or dreams (cf. Acts 2:17). The diviner extracted hidden intelligence from the handling of *things*—augury, the casting of lots (like the Urim and Thummim approved by the postexilic Priestly lawcode, cf. Exod 28:30, Lev 8:8, etc.); in passages like Isa 3:2 and Ezek 13:9 there is no intimation that anything was wrong with diviners as such but only that they were falsifying the readings of their "tea-leaves." At this stage, in other words, Micah is only condemning prophecy that is false; he has not prejudged it to be false because of the medium by which it was derived. Far more, he has not tried to explain how true prophecy is given.

THE END OF JERUSALEM
3:9-12

> ⁹ Hear this, you heads of the house of Jacob
>   and rulers of the house of Israel,
>   who abhor justice and pervert all equity,
> ¹⁰ who build Zion with blood
>   and Jerusalem with wrong.
> ¹¹ Its heads give judgment for a bribe,
>   its priests teach for hire,
>   its prophets divine for money;
>   yet they lean upon the Lord and say,
>   "Is not the Lord in the midst of us?
>   No evil shall come upon us."
> ¹² Therefore because of you
>   Zion shall be plowed as a field;
>   Jerusalem shall become a heap of ruins,
>   and the mountain of the house a wooded height.

In v 11 we are given a clue as to what is the precise indictment that Micah wants to present against the leaders of Judah. They, the "heads of the house" and "rulers" who "abhor justice" and "pervert all equity," "who build Zion with blood and Jerusalem with wrong" (meaning that they have squeezed the slender resources of their victims by nothing short of bloodshed to provide the brick and mortar for their flamboyant municipal works) are precisely those who "give judgment for a bribe." As in Amos 5:10-17, the main culprits would appear to be those who hold in their hands the judicial and administrative reins of justice and who have permitted themselves to be bought by whoever would pay the price, perverting their office in cynical disregard of the commonweal.

Allied with them, or at least equally guilty with them in the abuse of their powers are those other two familiar exponents of institutional authority, the priests and the prophets. As before, there is no condemnation here of institutions as such or even of the propriety of professional fees. What is involved is the more than subtle difference between accepting pay for one's services and letting out one's self for hire. Priests and prophets who have made themselves hirelings will teach and prophesy precisely what their employers want to hear. So arrogant are these pillars of society in their possession of power that they identify their wants with what ought to be their wonts: in their minds the very fact that they do what they do is the guarantee that it is what should be done. They and their presence testify that Yahweh is with them and that therefore no evil can befail them. "God is on our side." Alas, there is no such guarantee. To the contrary, their continued place in power is the proof that the glorious city of Jerusalem, so confident in its present state of prosperity, shall soon become a total devastation.

THE ESCHATOLOGICAL ZION
4:1-4

> **4** It shall come to pass in the latter days that the mountain of the house of the Lord

shall be established as the highest of the mountains
and shall be raised up above the hills;
and peoples shall flow to it,
2 and many nations shall come, and say:
"Come, let us go up to the mountain
of the Lord,
to the house of the God of Jacob;
that he may teach us his ways
and we may walk in his paths."
For out of Zion shall go forth the law,
and the word of the Lord from Jerusalem.
3 He shall judge between many peoples, and shall
decide for strong nations afar off;
and they shall beat their swords into plowshares,
and their spears into pruning hooks;
nation shall not lift up sword against nation,
neither shall they learn war any more;
4 but they shall sit every man under his vine
and under his fig tree,
and none shall make them afraid;
for the mouth of the Lord of hosts has spoken.

From this point on, we are concerned with a good deal
of prophetic material that can hardly be the work of the
eighth-century prophet whose name stands at the head of
this book. Proportionately, there is much more of this
kind of material in the Book of Micah than in the Books of
Amos and Hosea. For whatever reason, the postexilic redactors of Israel's prophetic literature have been particularly active in this work. There are also authentically Mican
words here, or at least words which may as easily belong to
Micah as to anyone else. At all events, everything that
follows is part of the precious heritage of the prophetic
tradition of the Old Testament.

We begin with some beautiful verses, the first three of

which are almost identical with Isa 2:2-4, regarding the eschatological Jerusalem, while the fourth, an old complacent Israelite proverb, parallels Zech 3:10. In times past it was a favorite pastime of critics to debate with which of the prophets these passages were "original" and who, in turn, had borrowed them from whom. Now it is more reasonably recognized that these were traditional cadences which Israelite authors could employ as common property, just as modern authors constantly make use of "familiar sayings." They are, in this acceptation, timeless and anonymous.

Thus the statement about the eschatological Jerusalem, appropriately inserted here to redress the picture of the utter devastation of Jerusalem painted by Micah in the preceding chapter. There was ample precedent (in Psalms 120-134, for example, and in excursions like those of Pss 49:3, 89:13) for this mystical portrayal of a future Jerusalem that would be the center of all the nations when the Lord at last would put an end to all wars and strife and bring about his own reign of idyllic peace. Fitting indeed that the house of the Lord which Micah had decreed a rubble (3:12) should in the ideal future be a house of instruction for the whole world that all might know the ways of God! The rather modest and bourgeois vision of the ideal in v 4 tempers considerably the grandiose imagery of the eschatology of vv 1-3 (cf. 1 Kgs 5:5, 2 Kgs 18:31) and has the virtue of directing the viewer's sight to the solid Israelite earth of reality. All in all, the vision is of "the latter days" (v 1), the end-time which is not Micah's purview.

YAHWEH AND THE GODS
4:5

> [5] For all the peoples walk
> each in the name of its god,

but we will walk in the name of the
Lord our God
for ever and ever.

A puzzling verse. It is asserted—by whom and for whom?—that while the Gentiles have their several gods, the God for Israel is only Yahweh, in whose name alone and according to whose ways alone Israel may "walk." Perhaps it is simply a pious and hopeful resolution that was felt called for by the preceding context. The nations which in the final days will seek to learn the ways of Yahweh now wander in the name of other gods. Only if Israel is faithful to its destiny can it ever become that light to the Gentiles which will emanate from Zion.

THE RECOVERY OF ZION
4:6-8

⁶ In that day, says the Lord,
    I will assemble the lame
    and gather those who have been driven away,
    and those whom I have afflicted;
⁷ and the lame I will make the remnant;
    and those who were cast off, a strong nation;
    and the Lord will reign over them in Mount Zion
    from this time forth and for evermore.
⁸ And you, O tower of the flock,
    hill of the daughter of Zion,
    to you shall it come,
    the former dominion shall come,
    the kingdom of the daughter of Jerusalem.

This passage, too, concerns a happy future of Jerusalem, though not a future quite as remote as that of vv 1-4 above. The verses belong to a time far later than Micah's in the eighth century (the time of Micah is "the former do-minion" of v 8), to the time rather of the exilic age of the sixth century when prophets were proclaiming the end of Judah's travail and that once again the Lord would reign in Zion and Israel would be restored. Such is also the mes-sage of the Second Isaiah.

EXILE
4:9-10

⁹ Now why do you cry aloud?
   Is there no king in you?
   Has your counselor perished,
   that pangs have seized you like a woman in travail?
¹⁰ Writhe and groan, O daughter of Zion,
   like a woman in travail;
   for now you shall go forth from the city
   and dwell in the open country;
   you shall go to Babylon.
   There you shall be rescued,
   there the Lord will redeem you
   from the hand of your enemies.

Quite different is the tone of these verses: the only con-textual connection with the preceding is that the prophetic author continues to speak of Jerusalem. The verses refer to an Israel (Judah) about to go into exile, its leaders having failed it, its present prospect only one of agony. There is, however, this ray of hope, that the experience of defeat and exile will be remedial, and that the Lord will eventually redeem Israel from the toils of its enemies. Such was the message that Jeremiah was to send to the exiles in Babylonia (cf. Jer 29:1-23). As v 10 shows, this passage too belongs to the Babylonian period of Jeremiah rather than to the Assyrian age of Micah.

THE SIEGE OF JERUSALEM
4:11-5:1

¹¹ Now many nations
are assembled against you,
saying, "Let her be profaned,
and let our eyes gaze upon Zion."
¹² But they do not know
the thoughts of the Lord,
they do not understand his plan,
that he has gathered them as sheaves
to the threshing floor.
¹³ Arise and thresh,
O daughter of Zion,
for I will make your horn iron
and your hoofs bronze;
you shall beat in pieces many peoples,
and shall devote their gain to the Lord,
their wealth to the Lord of the whole earth.
5 Now you are walled about with a wall;
siege is laid against us;
with a rod they strike upon the cheek
the ruler of Israel.

These are vv 11-14 of chap. 4 in the Hebrew text.

Again Jerusalem, and again Jerusalem in trouble; but this time we have a passage that can easily be Micah's. It speaks of "many nations" being assembled against Jerusalem, an expression which fits very well into the description of the Assyrian incursions (cf. Isa 17:12). Zion is exhorted to defy its enemies, an injunction for which there is other precedent in classical prophecy (cf. 2 Kgs 19:21-31= Isa 37:22-32), even on the part of prophets who like Micah and Isaiah were most censorious of Israel's shortcomings and recognized as divine chastisement what would be visited upon it through foreign invasion and pillage. The background of 5:1 can be best clarified, perhaps, in terms of the invasion of Judah in 701 B.C. by the Assyrian king Sennacherib who, according to his own annals, "shut up [the Judahite king] Hezekiah like a bird in a cage" in his city of Jerusalem. (Sennacherib's triumphalist language glosses over an admission that he was unable to capture the city, which had been his objective.) The Israelite version of these events is to be found in 2 Kings 18-19 and Isaiah 36-37. These verses remind us, and sometimes we need the reminder, of the solidarity and empathy which the prophets felt for their own society, however critically they judged it.

THE MESSIAH
5:2-6

> ² But you, O Bethlehem Ephrathah,
>   who are little to be among the clans of Judah,
>   from you shall come forth for me
>   one who is to be ruler in Israel,
>   whose origin is from of old,
>   from ancient days.
> ³ Therefore he shall give them up until the time
>   when she who is in travail has brought forth;
>   then the rest of his brethren shall return
>   to the people of Israel.
> ⁴ And he shall stand and feed his flock
>   in the strength of the Lord,
>   in the majesty of the name of the Lord his God.
>   And they shall dwell secure, for now he shall be great
>   to the ends of the earth.
> ⁵ And this shall be peace,
>   when the Assyrian comes into our land
>   and treads upon our soil,

> that we will raise against him seven shepherds
> and eight princes of men;
>
> 6 they shall rule the land of Assyria with the sword,
> and the land of Nimrod with the drawn sword;
> and they shall deliver us from the Assyrian
> when he comes into our land
> and treads within our border.

These verses are 5:1-5 in the Hebrew text. Similarly, the remaining verses of chap. 5 are, in the *RSV,* one ahead of the Hebrew enumeration and the enumeration of other English versions of the Hebrew.

For the same reasons that we advanced above, we find no difficulty in ascribing to Micah this particular passage. A prophet of Israel was attuned to all the authentic traditions of his people and religion, the favorable as well as the unfavorable. Just as Micah could join with Isaiah in throwing defiance in the teeth of his people's enemies in virtue of a divine promise that would eventually prevail, so we can easily imagine his sharing Isaiah's Judahistic messianic expectation, though in his own very special way.

Not everything in these verses is certain. The explicit word "Bethlehem" may be, in part, an explicative gloss on the text, though there is no doubt that it was Bethlehem to which Micah was referring. Isaiah's messianism was rooted in the traditions of Jerusalem, the city that David had made his own. Micah, the countryman, abandons Jerusalem and harks back to an earlier stage of the Davidic saga. Thus the tiny village of Bethlehem is contrasted with the great city of Jerusalem. Everything that Jerusalem is, Bethlehem is not. Christian tradition has contributed its own mystique to Bethlehem, but even in Jewish times (cf. Ruth 1:2, 4:11) Bethlehem had already been identified with Ephrathah as the birthplace of the great king David. A further step would have been to decree Bethlehem the place of origin of the Messiah, as Matt 2:5-6 has it.

All that Micah is saying here, however, the burden of his contrast of the city Jerusalem with the village Bethlehem, is that the latter is symbolic of an ancient guarantee ("whose origin is from of old, from ancient days") of a Davidic succession (2 Sam 7:11a-16) which in turn is the surety of the eventual salvation of a people (Psalm 89). Verse 3 is obscure, but there seems to be an allusion to Isa 7:14, part of an oracle given by the prophet Isaiah in a similar context of national peril. For a time undefined Israel must be delivered over to suffering until, finally, that leader will appear who will fulfill the ancient ideals associated with kingship and make justice and righteousness prevail. Verse 4 expresses those ideals with the traditional language of a "royal" psalm like Psalm 72, which details them at much greater length.

If the preceding verse about the besieged ruler of Israel (5:1) did, in fact, refer to Hezekiah, then it is obvious that Micah did not look to Hezekiah to fulfill the kingly ideal of which we have been speaking, contrary to what Isaiah may once have done. In the concluding vv 5-6 of this passage, however, the realization of this ideal seems to be envisioned as coming relatively soon, with the termination of the Assyrian crisis. At this time, of course, there was not yet in Israelite expectation the notion of a once-for-all eschatological king-messiah, and every generation could always hope that the age-old aspirations entertained of the Davidic promise would finally find some kind of realization in its own generation. Furthermore, these verses seem to look to a collectivity of saviors ("seven shepherds," "eight princes of men") rather than to a single one in whom confidence is to be placed for triumph over the Assyrians.

THE REMNANT OF JACOB
5:7-9

> [7] Then the remnant of Jacob shall be
> in the midst of many peoples
> like dew from the Lord,
> like showers upon the grass,
> which tarry not for men
> nor wait for the sons of men.
> [8] And the remnant of Jacob shall be among the nations,
> in the midst of many peoples,
> like a lion among the beasts of the forest,
> like a young lion among the flocks of sheep,
> which, when it goes through, treads down
> and tears in pieces, and there is none to deliver.
> [9] Your hand shall be lifted up over your adversaries,
> and all your enemies shall be cut off.

As with 4:6-8 above, we seem to be dealing here with a prophetic passage dating from the time of the exile, when the remnants of Israel, those who had survived the debacles of both north and south, were literally scattered among the nations of the earth. Prophetic consolations of this kind strengthened the resolve of the people during this time of degradation one day to recover their identity on their own land after the destruction of their enemies. Though perhaps in not quite so triumphalistic a fashion, their hopes were eventually to be realized, and prophecy did not disappoint.

THE DIVINE WRATH
5:10-15

> [10] And in that day, says the Lord,
> I will cut off your horses from among you

and will destroy your chariots;
¹¹ and I will cut off the cities of your land
and throw down all your strongholds;
¹² and I will cut off sorceries from your hand,
and you shall have no more soothsayers;
¹³ and I will cut off your images
and your pillars from among you,
and you shall bow down no more
to the work of your hands;
¹⁴ and I will root out your Asherim from among you
and destroy your cities.
¹⁵ And in anger and wrath I will execute vengeance
upon the nations that did not obey.

With these verses we are once again on terrain that can readily by Micah's. They are concerned with matters that coincide with his interests, and they are perfectly compatible with eighth-century prophecy, his included.

What they do is systematically and in series knock down the supposed props on which Israel has relied for survival in preference to putting its trust in its Maker and the giver of its way of life. These props are, first of all, Israel's fighting forces and fortified cities (cf. Hos 1:7, 14:3). These shall be swept aside utterly. Even more importantly, Israel shall be deprived of the religious talismans in which it has trusted. Some of these the prophet doubtless regarded as unredeemable on any score, while others had merely been made the occasion of vain belief and misplaced confidence. "Sorceries" and "soothsayers" refer to the soothing, beguiling activities of the false prophets who out of cynical greed or their proclivity for wish-fulfillment encouraged nationalist bravado and groundless self-confidence. Somewhat later on when the inevitability of Judah's humiliation was apparent to all but the most obtuse, Jeremiah had to enveigh against the same breed of charlatans who were deluding their compatriots with visions of glory instead of shame (Jer 27:9-10). Finally, there are other appurtenances of vain observance—images, sacred pillars, fetish figures (probably the Asherim of our text). This is standard prophetic language in condemnation of idolatry.

The final verse of this section may be more pregnant with meaning than is immediately apparent. Most everyone agrees that in it the vision of divine judgment extends beyond Israel to embrace as well the Gentile nations *(goyim)* who are equally guilty of wrong. What is not so obvious is that by this extension in this context the prophet is insinuating that in his wrath Yahweh will deal with his own people no differently than he would with a nation of Gentiles (cf. Amos 9:7).

ISRAEL AT THE BAR OF JUSTICE
6:1-8

6   Hear what the Lord says:
Arise, plead your case before the mountains,
and let the hills hear your voice.
² Hear, you mountains, the controversy
of the Lord,
and you enduring foundations of the earth;
for the Lord has a controversy with his people,
and he will contend with Israel.
³ "O my people, what have I done to you?
In what have I wearied you? Answer me!
⁴ For I brought you up from the land of Egypt,
and redeemed you from the house of bondage;
and I sent before you Moses, Aaron, and Miriam.
⁵ O my people, remember what Balak king of Moab
devised,
and what Balaam the son of Beor answered him,

> and what happened from Shittim to Gilgal,
>   that you may know the saving acts of the Lord."
> 6 "With what shall I come before the Lord,
>   and bow myself before God on high?
>   Shall I come before him with burnt offerings,
>   with calves a year old?
> 7 Will the Lord be pleased with thousands of rams,
>   with ten thousands of rivers of oil?
>   Shall I give my first-born for my transgression,
>   the fruit of my body for the sin of my soul?"
> 8 He has showed you, O man, what is good;
>   and what does the Lord require of you
>   but to do justice, and to love kindness,
>   and to walk humbly with your God?

In times past some critics were skeptical about the Mican authorship of this passage, largely because they thought its literary qualities somewhat above the attainments of which a rustic Judahite was supposed to be capable. The judgment was highly subjective, of course, and presupposed the critics' familiarity with the private ways of a prophet to whom they had never even been properly introduced. Besides all that, we now recognize that the passage has made use of set formulas and traditional liturgical language that was as much at the disposal of a Micah as it was to any other alert Judahite of the time. The content is appropriate to the era of Micah as it is not to a later one. These verses form probably the best and the most complete exemplification in the prophetic literature of the *rîb* (the word translated here "controversy," which actually means "litigation"), the prophetic lawsuit, as it has been called.

We must figure the prophet himself as the first speaker, acting in the capacity of the Lord's messenger or advocate. He announces the *rîb,* inviting Yahweh to plead his case and at the same time summoning the attention of the "tribunal," which is the cosmos itself (cf. 1:2 above and also Isa 1:2).

In vv 3-5 we have the Lord's plea, which takes the form of a recital of all his beneficences throughout Israel's history (v 5, "saving acts," literally "justices" = "righteous deeds"). Implied, of course, though not stated, is the *in re* of the case in which Yahweh is plaintiff and Israel the defendant: the base ingratitude which Israel has shown, its miserable failure to reciprocate Yahweh's righteous ways by the righteous conduct of a people whom he has identified with himself. Has he done Israel harm? he asks rhetorically. Rather, from exodus through the wilderness to the entry into the land of promise (cf. Exodus and Numbers *passim;* Joshua 1-4), has he not lavished on Israel protection, tender care, saving presence? We are reminded here of Amos 2:9-11.

In vv 6-7 the people reply. We must imagine, contrary to what, unfortunately, usually occurs in confrontations of this kind, that they are touched to repentance, leading to their request for prophetic enlightenment concerning the way they should go about making amends for their breach of contract. Animal sacrifices and libations are not the answer. We know the prophetic attitude towards these rites, which was to regard them as tolerable only when they were sacramental of internal conviction, pernicious when they were empty gestures which had usurped its place. It is somewhat fascinating to find human sacrifice, the offering up of the first-born, taking pride of place in this list of religious practices suggested as possibly pleasing to the Lord. Officially, this dread ritual was banned in Israel as an abomination (cf. Deut 12:31), but we know that it was in fact practiced by Israelites before and after Micah's time (cf. 1 Kgs 16:34, 2 Kgs 16:3, 21:6); in the Jerusalem of Jeremiah, the practice seems to have become almost endemic (cf. Jer 7:31). What is fascinating is that this revolting act can be mentioned so matter-of-factly by people and prophet together as just another option which a highly religious nation thought it possessed as a means of honoring its Deity. Perhaps nowhere else in the Bible has it been brought out more poignantly how inhumane and evil religion can become—even a certifiably "good" religion—when it is severed from its roots and bent to the service of alien values, whether these be national, racial, economic, or social.

In contrast, v 8 contains one of those perfect summations of biblical religion that we frequently encounter in the prophets. It should not be necessary to point out that the "man" addressed in this verse, the Hebrew *adam,* is generic, signifying the human person male and female. It may be worthy of observation, however, that in this context of Yahwistic prophecy there is a particular connotation for this "man," since he denotes the universality of the human condition. The moral will of the God of Israel revealed in its experience and history is a universal code of conduct for the entire human race and no mere sectarian law. That revelation is here expressed by the "justice" featured by Amos, the elusive *ḥesed* favored by Hosea, here aptly rendered "kindness," and by an expression proper to Micah: "walk humbly with your God." The combination manages nicely to indicate the relation of the social virtues to the God-man connection which is religion.

THE CRIMES OF JERUSALEM
6:9-16

> [9] The voice of the Lord cries to the city—
>   and it is sound wisdom to fear thy name:
>   "Hear, O tribe and assembly of the city!
> [10] Can I forget the treasures of wickedness in the house

of the wicked,
and the scant measure that is accursed?
[11] Shall I acquit the man with wicked scales
and with a bag of deceitful weights?
[12] Your rich men are full of violence;
your inhabitants speak lies,
and their tongue is deceitful in their mouth.
[13] Therefore I have begun to smite you,
making you desolate because of your sins.
[14] You shall eat, but not be satisfied,
and there shall be hunger in your inward parts;
you shall put away, but not save,
and what you save I will give to the sword.
[15] You shall sow, but not reap;
you shall tread olives, but not anoint yourselves with oil;
you shall tread grapes, but not drink wine.
[16] For you have kept the statutes of Omri,
and all the works of the house of Ahab;
and you have walked in their counsels;
that I may make you a desolation,
and your inhabitants a hissing;
so you shall bear the scorn of the peoples."

There verses have been considerably edited, but there is
no reason to suspect that their substance does not derive
from the eighth-century Judahite prophet Micah to whom
tradition has ascribed them. Even v 16 which accuses the
targets of this prophecy of carrying out and imitating the
principles of Omri and Ahab does not militate against this
conclusion. Similarly Ezekiel (cf. Ezekiel 23, for example)
would later speak of Judah as having taken the deplorable
example of the northern kingdom only as an object of em-
ulation, to be surpassed in fact. At the same time, it must
be admitted that this verse could be the result of Deutero-
nomistic editing. In any case, the prophecy is directed

against the "tribe and assembly of the city," by which are doubtless meant, respectively, Judah and Jerusalem. (This reading depends on a probable emendation of the Hebrew text: this is one of those frequent sections of Micah where verbal transmission has been less than perfect.)

In vv 10-15 we are reminded most especially of Amos 4-5, both in the specification of Judah's vices and in the terms of its retribution (note, for example, Amos 5:11-12). Micah's list of abominations reads like Amos': heaped up treasures (v 10a; Amos 3:10), false measures and lying weights to defraud the poor (vv 10b-11; Amos 8:4-6); the conspiracy of the rich and powerful to destroy their defenseless neighbors with every means at their disposal, including perjury (v 12; Amos 2:6-8). Prophetic judgment of north and south seems to have varied little, a testimony alike to the common frailty of the peoples to whom the prophets were missioned, but also, perhaps, to the single-mindedness of the prophetic religion.

LAMENTATION
7:1-7

7 Woe is me! For I have become
　　as when the summer fruit has been gathered,
　　as when the vintage has been gleaned:
　　there is no cluster to eat,
　　no first-ripe fig which my soul desires.
² The godly man has perished from the earth,
　　and there is none upright among men;
　　they all lie in wait for blood,
　　and each hunts his brother with a net.
³ Their hands are upon what is evil, to do it diligently;
　　the prince and the judge ask for a bribe,
　　and the great man utters the evil desire of his soul;
　　thus they weave it together.

⁴ The best of them is like a brier,
　the most upright of them a thorn hedge.
　The day of their watchmen, of their punishment, has
　come;
　now their confusion is at hand.
⁵ Put no trust in a neighbor,
　have no confidence in a friend;
　guard the doors of your mouth
　from her who lies in your bosom;
⁶ for the son treats the father with contempt,
　the daughter rises up against her mother,
　the daughter-in-law against her mother-in-law;
　a man's enemies are the men of his own house.
⁷ But as for me, I will look to the Lord,
　I will wait for the God of my salvation;
　my God will hear me.

If the preceding section reminded us of Amos, certainly this present one evokes Jeremiah (cf. especially Jer 8:22-9:6). It is the breakdown and disintegration of society that is in question here. However, as Jeremiah frequently does and Amos much less frequently, Micah is able in these verses to empathize with and to recognize himself to be a part with the people whom he has been sent to judge and to condemn. Their fate is his fate: all about him he sees in shambles the old ordinances and values that had held society together in his youth. Now these are all gone, and he no longer condemns but simply observes and deplores their passing. The particulars we have already seen, and they need no further rehearsal. Is there any point in trying to discover Micah in all of this?

Probably so. In v 7 the prophet who has previously identified himself with his people now suddenly distances himself by throwing himself upon the mercy of the God of his salvation. We are at a stage—which Jeremiah and Ezekiel would shortly proclaim as dogma—when, for better or for worse, the individual destiny could be separated from that of the people through "personal" religion. There is no certain guarantee, of course. The prophet merely hopes that God will hear him and not include him in the final disaster. It is not a particularly heroic plea, but it is probably the last authentic word that we have from Micah.

THE RECOVERY OF ZION
7:8-10

> [8] Rejoice not over me, O my enemy;
>   when I fall, I shall rise;
>   when I sit in darkness,
>   the Lord will be a light to me.
> [9] I will bear the indignation of the Lord
>   because I have sinned against him,
>   until he pleads my cause
>   and executes judgment for me.
>   He will bring me forth to the light;
>   I shall behold his deliverance.
> [10] Then my enemy will see,
>   and shame will cover her who said to me,
>   "Where is the Lord your God?"
>   My eyes will gloat over her;
>   now she will be trodden down
>   like the mire of the streets.

The final sections of the Book of Micah are undoubtedly supplement to the work of the eighth-century prophet attached to it by the postexilic redactors who followed a customary pattern of concluding these works with oracles of salvation and consolation. The woes of Israel had come and gone; now was the time for rebuilding on new hopes.

Who speaks here? It is evidently Jerusalem/Judah, acknowledging the depth of its guilt and the rightness of the judgment passed against it, but now confident of God's deliverance. And who is the "enemy" which is adjured not to gloat over Judah's downfall but rather to look to its own coming ruin? The word "enemy" is a feminine, obviously referring to another nation or group of nations. If the period of this prophecy is the time of Judah's final conquest by the Chaldeans (586 B.C.), as it probably is, the enemy is doubtless Edom which then stood by cheering on the Babylonian conquerors and did not hesitate to plunder what was left of the defenceless land (cf. Ps 137:7, Isa 63:1-6, etc.). As a matter of fact, Edom was destined for a national fate far more dismal than that of Judah in defeat. Judah regained its identity at about the same time that Edom was losing its own finally and utterly through foreign incursions which scattered it and left it without even a name.

THE REBUILDING OF ZION
7:11-13

> [11] A day for the building of your walls!
> In that day the boundary shall be far extended.
> [12] In that day they will come to you,
> from Assyria to Egypt,
> and from Egypt to the River,
> from sea to sea and from mountain to mountain.
> [13] But the earth will be desolate
> because of its inhabitants,
> for the fruit of their doings.

Again there is a prophecy of weal for Jerusalem, though of a later date: "A day for the building of your walls!" The time can hardly be other than about 445 B.C., the twentieth year of the Persian king Artaxerxes I, when authorization was given for the restoration of the devastated city (cf. Nehemiah 2-4). In prophetic chronology, we are in the period when the messianic expectations of the postexilic prophets Haggai and Zechariah had been dashed, when it had become apparent that whatever were the salvific designs of God, they would be achieved through some other means than a restored Davidic dynasty. One alternative that appealed to some prophetic spirits, like this one, was the city of Jerusalem itself, whose rebirth was viewed as a sign of Yahweh's eventual universal domination, in keeping with the mystique that had long attached to the holy city of David (see Ps 147:1-6, Mic 4:1-4, Zech 14:16-21, etc.). This kind of thinking was a presage of the "heavenly Jerusalem" concept which was taken up by later Jewish and early Christian thought to epitomize the reign of God in the world.

ZION'S PRAYER
7:14-20

¹⁴ Shepherd thy people with thy staff,
the flock of thy inheritance,
who dwell alone in a forest
in the midst of a garden land;
let them feed in Bashan and Gilead
as in the days of old.
¹⁵ As in the days when you came out of
the land of Egypt
I will show them marvelous things.
¹⁶ The nations shall see and be ashamed
of all their might;
they shall lay their hands on their mouths;
their ears shall be deaf;
¹⁷ they shall lick the dust like a serpent,
like the crawling things of the earth;
they shall come trembling out of their strongholds,

they shall turn in dread to the Lord our God,
and they shall fear because of thee.
[18] Who is a God like thee, pardoning iniquity
and passing over transgression
for the remnant of his inheritance?
He does not retain his anger for ever
because he delights in steadfast love.
[19] He will again have compassion upon us,
he will tread our iniquities under foot.
Thou wilt cast all our sins
into the depths of the sea.
[20]Thou wilt show faithfulness to Jacob
and steadfast love to Abraham,
as thou hast sworn to our fathers
from the days of old.

The final section of the Book of Micah is a psalm of confidence, a prayer of praise and impetration, a literary form with which we are familiar both from the Psalter and from the prophetic literature. Theoretically, it could belong to any period of Israel's history when it felt called upon to invoke its God in circumstances of national urgency. Practically, by context and content, it must be referred to the same postexilic age to which the surrounding verses belong.

First, the prophet/psalmist asks for God to deal with his people as he has dealt of old. Restoration is not a new experience; it is rather a continuation of the divine beneficence that has accompanied Israel from the beginning. Characteristically, the "motivation" offered to God to be now a shepherd and savior of his people is the simple fact that he has been such a shepherd and savior before. God's prior blessings have committed him to further and greater ones: he must continue to be what he has revealed himself to be (vv 14-15; in v 15b "show us" would be a better rendering of the text than the "I will show them" of *RSV).*

A further "motivation" to Yahweh is the resultant discomfiture of the Gentiles who will recognize in Israel's restoration the triumph of its God over their own (vv 16-17). At the same time, it will be an opportunity for them to acknowledge that the Yahweh of Israel is God indeed. In this postexilic age Israel was sensitive to a mission to proselytize, to communicate its higher vision of God and religion to other peoples. For whatever reasons, a later Judaism abandoned that mission and even repudiated it, more or less at the same time that the universalistic religion of Christianity was emerging and separating from it.

The final verses simply express their faith in the grace and mercy of the Lord despite all human transgression. They are one of the most engaging endings that have been devised for any of the prophetical books. No aid and comfort are offered to sinners: God "pardons" iniquity and "passes over" transgressions because he is a very special God who does this in view of a worthy remnant of the people which he is resolved to save. He does not exact justice by the inexorable rules of what man has determined to be just, "because he delights in *ḥesed*" (v 18a). Therefore the prophet can be secure in his faith (vv 19-20) that Israel will be redeemed, its sins forgotten, in keeping with promises made without condition to its fathers of old. In a somewhat later era a somewhat different Jew would take up this theme in a somewhat other fashion:

> Abraham "believed God, and it was reckoned to him as righteousness." So you see that it is men of faith who are the sons of Abraham. And the scripture, foreseeing that God would justify the Gentiles by faith, preached the gospel beforehand to Abraham, saying, "In you shall all the nations be blessed." So then, those who are men of faith are blessed with Abraham who had faith (Gal 3:6-9).

But that is the story of another prophet.

Some Suggested Reading

1. The general and particular introductions and commentaries in *The Jerome Biblical Commentary.*

2. John F. Craghan, C.SS.R., "Mari and its Prophets," *Biblical Theology Bulletin* 5 (1975) 32-55.

3. R. B. Y. Scott, *The Relevance of the Prophets* (New York: Macmillan, 1968).

4. Hans Walter Wolff, *Joel and Amos* (Hermeneia; Philadelphia: Fortress, 1977).

5. James L. Mays, *Amos. A Commentary* (Old Testament Library), London: SCM Press, 1976.

6. Robert B. Coote, *Amos among the Prophets: Composition and Theology* (Philadelphia: Fortress, 1981).

7. Hans Walter Wolff, *Hosea* (Hermeneia; Philadelphia: Fortress, 1974).

8. Francis I. Andersen and David Noel Freedman, *Hosea* (Anchor Bible; Garden City, NY: Doubleday, 1980).

9. James L. Mays, *Hosea. A Commentary* (Old Testament Library), London: SCM Press, 1969.

10. L. C. Allen, *The Books of Joel, Obadiah, Jonah and Micah* (Grand Rapids: Eerdmans, 1977).

11. Hans Walter Wolff, *The Prophet Micah* (Philadelphia: Fortress, 1981).

12. James L. Mays, *Micah. A Commentary* (Old Testament Library), London: SCM Press, 1976.

Some other publications
of
Michael Glazier, Inc.
1723 Delaware Avenue
Wilmington, Delaware 19806

NEW TESTAMENT MESSAGE
A Biblical-Theological Commentary
Editors: Wilfrid Harrington, O.P. & Donald Senior, C.P.

Individual volumes may be purchased separately
• **22 Volume Set, cloth edition $198**   • **22 Volume Set, paperback $119**

"A splendid new series . . . The aim is to mediate the finest of contemporary biblical scholarship to preachers, teachers, and students of the Bible . . . There are treasures to be found in every volume of it."

George MacRae, S.J.

"The stress is on the message, the good news, the *'God-Word'* of the Christian Scriptures."

The Bible Today

"A sane and well-informed series of commentaries which draws . . . on a wide range of modern biblical scholarship." *Henry Wansbrough, O.S.B.*

"This series offers new insights and rewards."

Sisters Today

". . . the series will be especially welcome to those who have benefited from William Barclay's series — and are now looking for something more."

Stephen Doyle, O.F.M.

"Belongs in the libraries of all Christian institutions and on the personal shelves of those whose professional task is teaching and preaching the Bible."

Dennis Hamm, S.J., Creighton University

GALILEE
From Alexander the Great to Hadrian
323 B.C.E. to 135 C.E.
by Seán Freyne

"It is a detailed, documented study that will probably be definitive on the subject."

Christianity Today

"His treatment is comprehensive, including chapters dealing *inter alia* with the geography of Galilee, the rise of Hellenism, Roman administration, the cities, social stratification, the attitude of Galilean Jewry towards the Jerusalem temple and halakhah, and the early development of Christianity."

Theological Studies

"The work is very thorough, fully documented, and a most valuable contribution to the study of early Judaism and early Christianity."

William Sanford LaSor, Fuller Theological Seminary

"The painstaking research, careful analyses, and cautious conclusions make it a model to follow for others similarly launching out into new territories. It will prove invaluable to New Testament scholars."

Christianity Today

Cloth $27.50

THE SAVING WORD
Sunday and Feastday Readings for the Liturgical Year

- Scriptural Commentary by Wilfrid Harrington, O.P.
- Patristic Readings by Thomas Halton
- Church Documents by Austin Flannery, O.P.

All who preach and pray the word of God can enrich the new liturgical year with a copy of *The Saving Word.*

What it contains

Theology Digest aptly describes its contents: "For each Sunday and feastday, it provides a biblical commentary; pertinent readings from the Fathers of the Church and other early Christian writings; and selections, directly related to the readings, from Vatican II and other post-conciliar documents."

Some comments on *The Saving Word* series

L'Observatore Romano: "If you are looking for a manageable up-to-date, dependable guide in the preparation of your Sunday sermon, treat yourself to a copy of *The Saving Word.* The basic arrangement is unique...A delight for the priest."

Rev. Andrew Greeley: "Perfectly splendid."

Bishop Thomas Mardaga: "*The Saving Word* is one of the best source books for the homilist."

Rev. John J. Greehy: "*The Saving Word* encourages us with basic materials to think through our sermons and not to insult the intelligence of our congregations."

Liturgical Year A, Year B, and Year C
Large paperback format...$10 each.

א